Missouri

OFF THE BEATEN PATH

THIRD EDITION

CATHY JOHNSON
AND
PATTI DeLANO

A Voyager Book

The Globe Pequot Press

Old Saybrook, Connecticut

To a friendship that withstood co-authorship;
to our fellow travelers Bob and Chris, and Harris;
and to Missouri—the Heart of America
and a great place to live.

Library of Congress Cataloging-in-Publication Data

Johnson, Cathy (Cathy A.)
Missouri : off the beaten path / by Cathy Johnson and
Patti DeLano.—3rd ed.
    p. cm. — (Off the beaten path series)
"A Voyager book."
Includes index.
ISBN 1-56440-887-6
1. Missouri—Guidebooks.   I. DeLano, Patti.   II. Title.
F464.3.J64   1996
917.7804'43—dc20   95-39754
                                                    CIP

Manufactured in the United States of America
Third Edition/First Printing

MISSOURI

NORTHWEST

NORTHEAST

CENTRAL

SOUTHEAST

SOUTHWEST

CONTENTS

ACKNOWLEDGMENTS

No book comes easily, but a sense of humor helps. It's especially true of a book of this sort, which requires so many hours of research and fine-tuning. The Missouri Tourism Bureau and the Missouri departments of conservation and natural resources, not to mention all the visitors' bureaus and chambers of commerce we contacted in hundreds of little towns, made it easier. We want to offer special thanks to the hundreds of people around the state who sent us new information and helped make the third edition even more fun.

It's impossible to include all the wonderful, quirky places we discovered in the course of researching this book—it would weigh five pounds. Others we simply did not know about; still others have recently appeared or, sadly, have gone out of business. If you know of a special place, or a change in an existing listing, please write the publishers so that we can add this information when we next update the book.

INTRODUCTION

Think of Missouri and a hundred images tumble forward like candy from a piñata. The Pony Express. The Santa Fe Trail. Lewis and Clark. The Civil War. Frank and Jesse James. Mark Twain (who once said that he was born here because "Missouri was an unknown new state and needed attractions"; we certainly got one in Samuel Clemens).

But all of the images are not from the distant past, flickering like a silent movie through the veil of time. There's Branson, now threatening Nashville as the country music capital of the country, with twenty-seven theaters and stars the magnitude of Johnny Cash and Andy Williams. (We'll tell you how to beat the crowds and traffic and help you find a quiet B&B instead of a computer-located motel.) There's also the Plaza, the world's first shopping center. Kansas City steaks. Charlie Parker and jazz. General John J. Pershing. The Gateway Arch. Barbecue. Writers Calvin Trillin and Richard Rhodes. Actors Kathleen Turner, Bob Cummings, John Goodman, and Don Johnson, as well as Walt Disney, all have ties to Missouri. And of course, our own Harry S Truman. Now you're on a roll.

What you may not think of immediately are the things we will show you in *Missouri: Off the Beaten Path*. Did you know that J.C. Penney got his start here? There's a museum to honor his modest beginnings in Hamilton. And Jacques Cousteau—when you think of the man, you imagine oceanic dives in faraway places, right? Not always. Cousteau filmed a "deep-earth dive" right here in Bonne Terre and explored his way up the Mississippi and Missouri rivers as well. Then there's the Kingdom of Callaway, with its postwar ties to none other than Winston Churchill. There are wineries and breweries and distilleries, and there are elegant restaurants and comfort-food cafes that range from fine French to fire-breathing Cajun, with home-style cooking settled somewhere in between.

What we are not is flat farmland, empty prairie, or wall-to-wall cows (or cowboys and Indians, for that matter). There's a rich diversity of landscape here.

Missouri is covered with forests and rolling hills. It boasts over 5,000 caves, and those are only the ones we know about. The rugged white bluffs along the rivers (the rocky remains of a prehistoric inland sea) and the volcanic formations and karst sinks in the Lake of the Ozarks area are among the most beautiful in the country. The rivers that sculpted all this spectacular scenery are magnets for exploration; the Jacks Fork, the Eleven Point, and the Current rivers are designated National Scenic Riverways. Remnant prairies still beckon—patchwork bits and pieces left over from presettlement days, when the big bluestem and gayfeather were tall enough to hide a man on horseback, and the wind-driven waves imitated a sea of grass.

The Mississippi River, which forms the eastern boundary of the state, is still one of the busiest shipping lanes in the world, and has been flowing here since before the dawn of time. The upstart Missouri River, on the other hand, was the gift of a departing glacier a short half million years ago; it simply wasn't there before that time. The division between the glaciated plains to the north (rolling and covered with a generous layer of topsoil, also a legacy of the wall of ice, which stole the soil from points north) and the bony Ozark region to the south (rough and hilly with valleys cut deep into rock) is the river that bisects the state from Kansas City to St. Louis. Missouri is where old prairie runs up against the oldest mountain range in the country—a fitting symbol for one of the most historically divided states in the Union.

It was in Missouri that the Civil War was most brutal, issuing as it did from tension that had been building for decades. This pre-Civil War strife between free-state Kansas and the Southern-leaning Missouri was bloody, especially because many Missourians believed that slavery was wrong and worked with the Underground Railroad to help slaves to freedom.

After the Civil War, Quantrill's Raiders and such legendary outlaws as Cole Younger and the James brothers continued the bloodshed. The state bears the reminders to this day. Civil War battlefields and tiny cemeteries, with their solemn testimony of the losses of the war, embody the lingering dichotomy between Northern and Southern sensibilities.

Before the Civil War and for some years afterward, the two rivers—the Missouri and the Mississippi—were main arteries of commerce. All of Missouri's large cities began as river ports with a lively competition between them for business and settlers. Kansas City and its popular hot spot, Westport (formerly Westport Landing); St. Joseph, Lexington, Boonville, and Jefferson City, the capital; and Hermann, Washington, and St. Charles, the first capital, all began as ports on the Missouri. Hannibal, St. Louis, Ste.

Genevieve, Cape Girardeau, and New Madrid were ports of call on the Mississippi.

Today the big rivers and their connecting waterway system make a 22,000-mile navigable network. Almost all year the tugs and barges can be seen wherever public and private docks allow commodities to be moved inexpensively by water. Only winter's ice jams stop the flow of traffic.

Kansas City, Missouri's second-largest city (now outgrowing St. Louis, much to the pride of the western part of the state) had its beginnings as a shipping point on the Kansas (called the Kaw) River bend of the Muddy Mo, where the river turns sharply east on its trek across the state's midriff. The region known by early explorers as the Big Blue Country was occupied by the Kanza (Kansas) Indians, whose name means "people of the south wind." The peaceful Kanza engaged in farming, fishing, and trapping; they were quickly displaced when settlers began to move in.

Missouri was once as far off the beaten path as one could get, the jumping-off point to the trackless West; beyond was the great unknown. You can still see the tracks of the wagon wheels etched deeply into our soil on the Santa Fe, California, and Oregon trails.

Now everything's up-to-date in Kansas City, as the lyrics to a song once told us. A beautifully modern metropolis, Kansas City has more fountains than any city except Rome and more miles of tree-lined boulevards than any other American city. The Nelson-Atkins Museum of Art owns one of the finest collections of Oriental art in the country.

St. Louis, on the other side of the state, has a world-class botanical garden and a rich cultural heritage that rivals any big city in the East. Not surprisingly, St. Louis is proud of its French legacy, a gift of the early explorers.

The KATY Trail (its name is derived from MKT, the Missouri-Kansas-Texas Railroad) begins nearby in Machens just north of St. Louis. This bicycle and hiking trail follows the old MKT railroad route to Sedalia 90 miles east of Kansas City. It will soon cover 200 miles of river bluffs, forests, and farmlands with cafes and shops along its route to cater to trail buffs.

The word Missouri first appeared on maps made by French explorers in the 1600s. It was the name of a group of Indians living near the mouth of a large river. Pekketanoui, roughly its Indian name, means "river of the big canoes," and the Missouri would have required them—it was big, swift, and tricky to navigate before the locks and dams of the U.S. Army Corps of Engineers tamed it, or attempted to.

We don't know how the native Americans pronounced Missouri, and it is about a fifty-fifty split among the state's current residents. In a recent survey a little more than half the population, most in western Missouri, pronounced the name "Missour-uh." The eastern half of the state favored "Missour-ee."

The "Show Me State" carries its nickname proudly. We have a reputation as stubborn individualists, as hardheaded as our own Missouri mules—or so they say—and we won't believe something until you show us. It's not such a bad way to be. Our people, like our agrarian ancestors, want concrete proof—we'll change, all right, but only when we're fully convinced that change is synonymous with progress, and that progress is indeed an improvement. The past is definitely worth preserving when it is as colorful as ours.

So we will show you parts of the Show Me State that are tucked away off the beaten path. Some are in the middle of farmland, some are in national forests, and some are in our largest cities. There will be no "Worlds of Fun" or "Six Flags Over Mid-America" or Royals' Stadium plugs in this book; such places are definitely on the path, and you can find them on your own. What this book does have is something for everyone, as out of the way—and "far from the madding crowd"—as you could wish.

No matter where you're from, whether you love a fine Bordeaux or a fine bourbon, whether you like to go in a sports car dressed to the nines, or in a pickup truck wearing an old pair of jeans, you will feel at home in Missouri.

The prices and rates listed in this guidebook were confirmed at press time. We recommend, however, that you call establishments before traveling to obtain current information.

SOUTHEAST MISSOURI

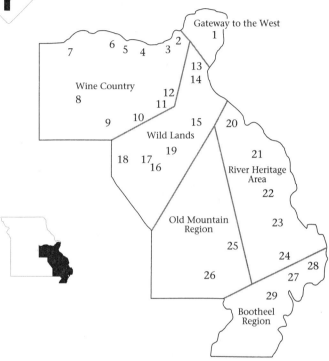

Gateway to the West

Wine Country

Wild Lands

River Heritage Area

Old Mountain Region

Bootheel Region

1. Blueberry Hill
2. Eureka
3. Hunter's Hollow Inn and Restaurant
4. not just Cut and Dried
5. Bias Vineyards & Winery
6. Hermannhoff Winery Festhalle
7. Birk's Gasthaus
8. Americana Antique, Art and Curio Shop
9. Ferrigno's Winery and B&B
10. Onondaga Cave
11. Meramec State Park Lodge
12. Jesse James Wax Museum
13. Mastodon State Park
14. Blue Owl Restaurant and Bakery
15. Bonne Terre Mines
16. Good Ole Days Country Store
17. Johnson Shut-ins
18. Dillard Mill State Historic Site
19. Elephant Rocks State Park
20. Southern Hotel
21. Tric's Family Restaurant
22. Iron Mountain Railway
23. Broussard's Cajun Restaurant
24. Lambert's Cafe
25. Mingo National Wildlife Refuge
26. Margaret Harwell Art Museum
27. Big Oak Tree State Park
28. Towosahgy State Historic Site
29. Hunter-Dawson Home and Historic Site

Southeast Missouri

To call southeast Missouri the most beautiful part of the state wouldn't be fair; beauty is a mysterious commodity based on personal definition, as intangible as smoke. But it has plenty to offer. There is natural beauty—dappled shade of the national forests, cascades of clear blue springs and rivers, and white river bluffs and volcanic rock formations of the Johnson Shut-ins— that meets everyone's definition of beauty. Antebellum and Victorian homes on wide boulevards grace the oldest cities west of the Mississippi. Both beautiful and historic, southeast Missouri will appeal to all your senses with its food, wine, scenery, and rich and varied past.

When the river was the frontier to the American West, thousands crossed it in search of land, freedom, and a new life. Trappers, traders, explorers, and settlers joined Native Americans in the fertile river valleys and rich prairies.

Enter the state from the east, and you will encounter the St. Louis area, the big city/small town that spreads west on Interstate 70 and south on Interstate 55. Sneak off of these two amazingly uncrowded freeways (uncrowded, at least, during nonrush hours) and the many small highways branching off from them to find some of the most charming towns in the state, towns that date back to the beginning of the westward expansion of the country.

Here, you have a choice of crowded festivals and busy public campgrounds or the isolation and peace deep in the national forests and wildlife preserves. Missouri in winter is quietly beautiful and secluded; in summer, it is lively and fun. Adventures here range from scuba diving (yes! deep-earth diving in Missouri!) and whitewater canoeing to wine tasting and genealogical searches in the oldest records in the American West. Whether you want to party or to get away from it all, you can wander off the beaten path into southeast Missouri.

Gateway to the West

The bustling St. Louis area is still the best place to begin westward exploration. Located on a shelf of riverfront under a bluff, the original city spread to the prairies surrounding it. It was the starting point for the Meriwether Lewis and William Clark expedition in 1804. The history of western expansion begins here where the Missouri and the Mississippi rivers meet.

St. Louis, founded in 1764, boasts the oldest park west of the Mississippi (Lafayette Park), the second-oldest symphony orchestra in the nation, the world's largest collection of mosaic art at the Cathedral of St. Louis, and one of the finest botanical gardens in the world. The graceful Italianate mansion, Tower Grove House at the Missouri Botanical Garden, blooms with color each Christmas season. Local garden clubs, the Herb Society of St. Louis and others bathe the house in wreaths, seasonal flowers, and greens. Candlelight tours and teas and holiday luncheons are the special events. The home and 79-acre garden are open for tours every day. Call (314) 577–5150 for more information.

Also in St. Louis are the futuristic Climatron, and the country's tallest man-made monument, the Gateway Arch, which is also the world's third most popular tourist attraction (but we're talking beaten path here, aren't we?)

It's also a city of firsts. The first Olympiad in the United States was held here in 1904; the first hot dog, ice-cream cone, and iced tea were all introduced at the 1904 World's Fair. Remember "Meet me in St. Louie, Louie, meet me at the fair?"

A great place to start exploring St. Louis is at 1900 Wyoming in historic Benton Park. This building, dating from 1893, now houses a one-stop market that sells anything a traveler might need. You'll find quality merchandise and a complete bed-and-breakfast reservation service.

One of the finest places to call home in this area is **Lemp's Landing** in Benton Park. This 1893 two-story townhouse is all yours and is popular among visiting CEOs and honeymooners in the St. Louis area. There is a kitchen on the main level, and the second level has bedrooms with king-sized beds and a two-person Jacuzzi. A bottle of champagne and breakfast are included for $125. For information call (314) 771–1993.

The Gateway to the West (or to the East if you are traveling the other way) was fed by train travel beginning in the early 1800s. More than 100,000 passengers passed through the station each day. (Actually, it sounds more like a revolving door than a gateway.)

The 100-year-old Union Station is a two-block-long gray limestone fortress with red-tiled roof. The clock tower looms 230 feet into the air. When the last train left the station in 1978, the city had a white elephant of gargantuan proportions on its hands. The station was too historic to tear down; too expensive to keep up. So, it received a new identity: it is a retail, restaurant, and entertainment complex whose 100 shops, cinema, restaurants, and night clubs are drawing tourists downtown again and sparking a revival of the area. There's even a virtual reality mini-arcade, called Virtuality, where you can slip on a helmet and join the cyberworld of Zone Hunter.

The Grand Hall, once the waiting room, is now the lobby of the 546–room Hyatt Regency hotel. Look up at the 65–foot barrel-vaulted ceilings and finely decorated walls. Arches and columns abound. The famous "whispering arch" allows you to whisper to a friend 40 feet away. Sculpted maidens holding gilded torches, floral flourishes, and scrollwork entice the eye. Most impressive is the glowing stained glass window depicting three women representing New York, San Francisco—and the one in the middle—St. Louis, the crossroads of America.

Downstairs is the Midway and cavernous Train Shed. More than 130 shops, cafes and restaurants surrounded by walkways, bridges, fountains and flowers, fill the space. On most weekends strolling mimes and jugglers entertain shoppers. Boats cruise on a manmade lake next to an open-air *biergarten*. And although the trains don't stop here anymore, you can grab the MetroLink public rail system right outside for a ride to the Gateway Arch or Busch Stadium.

First though, get a map of St. Louis. Although the many interesting little neighborhoods make it charming, it also makes it difficult for visitors.

The Gateway Arch may not be exactly off the beaten path—after all, it's one of the most-visited tourist destinations in the country—but did you know there's a wonderful museum tucked away underground beneath the Arch in the Jefferson National Expansion Memorial National Park? It's the Museum of Western Expansion, which documents our irrepressible urge to explore and settle lands ever farther westward. We didn't stop until we reached the Pacific Ocean; the museum makes you feel you were along for the trip. You'll see artifacts and displays that relate to the Lewis and Clark expedition, which was intended not only to find a trade route to the West but to discover the natural history of this new land encompassed by the Louisiana Purchase. You'll find Native American and pioneer artifacts as well, and when you come back out blinking into the sunshine you'll experience a moment of disorientation as you reenter the twentieth century.

The museum is accessible with a $2.00 National Park fee, and it's more than worth the cost (tram fee to the top of the Arch is a bit higher). Also under the Arch are a fine bookstore and gift shop run by the National Park Service; be prepared to take a bit of history home with you.

While you history-minded folk are in the neighborhood of the Arch, don't miss the Old Cathedral Museum visible just to the west and still in the Gateway Arch park. Here you'll find some of the finest (and oldest) ecclesiastical art in the country, with works by the Old Masters not uncommon. Documents dating back to the beginning of the cathedral as well as photographs on the building of the Arch are all part of the museum. If it's Sunday evening, you can attend Mass at the cathedral at 5:00 P.M.

The Old Cathedral Museum (314–231–3250) at 209 Walnut is open daily from 10:00 A.M. to 4:30 P.M.; there is a 25–cent admission charge.

If you visit the new **St. Louis Cathedral** on Lindell in the Central West End, look up to the heavens, or the ceiling in this case, and you will see the largest collection of mosaic art in the world.

Still in the downtown area (and the air of the past) is the **St. Louis Mercantile Library Association** at 510 Locust. If you admire the works of Missouri artist George Caleb Bingham, who captured our history on canvas, if you're awed by the accomplishments of George Catlin as he traveled among the tribes of Native Americans and painted them one by one, if you've wished you could see a painting by one of the famous Peale family of nineteenth-century artists (portrait painter Sarah Peale, in this case, who supported herself for many years here in the past century), you won't want to miss this place. Admission is free.

This is the oldest circulating library west of the Mississippi, and in addition to art, you can find rare books: Americana, westward expansion, river transportation, and so on.

The name doesn't tell you the reason for searching out this

place, but once you know, you will be a regular at the **Crown Candy Kitchen** just 1¼ miles north of the Arch at 1401 St. Louis Avenue where wonderful chocolate candy has been made since 1913. The main attraction here, however, is the city's oldest soda fountain. Owners Andy and Mike Karandzieff grew up here and the place has been in the family since their grandfather opened it almost 85 years ago. Nothing much has changed in their world- class milk shakes: homemade ice cream, milk, and your choice of syrups. If you want a "malted," you can have that, too. Of course, what is a milk shake without a chili dog? Andy and Mike can fix that up for you, no problem. The malted had 1,100 calories in it, so what difference will a little chili dog make in the big scheme of things, right? Oh yes, they still make fresh chocolate candy in the winter. Summer hours are Monday through Saturday from 10:30 A.M. to 10:00 P.M. and on Sunday from noon to 10:00 P.M. In the winter they close at 9:00 P.M. Call (314) 621–9650 for more information.

As long as we are talking about ice cream it's only fair to tell you about another favorite. This is the old 1950s walk-up kind of place with a packed parking lot. See a lot of people in bright yellow T-shirts? Lucky you; you have found **Ted Drewes Frozen Custard** at 6726 Chippewa. This place has been a St. Louis favorite since 1929 when Ted's father started the business. Drewes is known for the thickest shake anywhere (you can hold it upside down and the spoon and straw stay put), so thick ("how thick is it?") he calls it a "concrete," because it just won't shake. So thick the server wears a hard hat. These thick—very thick—shakes have mysterious names such as the "Cardinal Sin," named for the baseball team (fudge sauce and red cherries) or the "All Shook Up" (Elvis's favorite snack; peanut-butter cookies and banana). Hours are from 11:00 A.M. until a little after midnight seven days a week. For information call (314) 481–2652. There's a second location at 4224 South Grand (314–352–7376) if one wasn't enough. This time order the "Abaco Mocha," a tropical treat, or a "Foxtreat" with fudge sauce, raspberries, and macadamia nuts.

The *Admiral* was a rusty old riverboat that had been moored in the city since 1940. When riverboat gambling was legalized in Missouri a few years ago, the *Admiral* was born again. She underwent a $40 million renovation and became **The President**

Casino on the *Admiral*: her art deco splendor and 1,500 slots and gaming tables is something to behold. You can get off the beaten path (Leonore Sullivan Boulevard on the north lake of the Arch) and onto the river aboard this dockside casino for a $2.00 entry fee. There is a food court on the A deck for sandwiches and the St. Louie Restaurant with lunch (brunch on Sunday), and a prime rib dinner buffet for only $9.95. Call (800) 772–3647 for reservations.

St. Louis is the hometown of Chuck Berry, so you might be in the mood for some golden oldies. It seems only right that you should find your thrill on ❖ **Blueberry Hill.** This place will bring back a lot of memories if you are of a certain age. A real 45 rpm juke box with hundreds of rock 'n' roll and rhythm and blues titles dating from 1950 waits for your coins. All 2,000 selections are cross-indexed in a large notebook, and the dates are hand-written on the selection buttons to settle the arguments over who and when. Rock and Roll Beer, fabulous hamburgers, and the best rest-room graffiti in the state add to the feeling. There's an Elvis room and lots of Howdy Doody. Drinks are served from the 104–year-old mahogany bar from 11:00 to 1:30 A.M. six days a week (until midnight on Sunday). Oh, and look closely at the window display done by Linda Edwards. Sometimes the display pieces are alive. Owner Joe Edwards says he is a friend of Chuck Berry's, but the place is actually named after a Fats Domino song. Take the University City loop on the west edge of the city of St. Louis to 6504 Delmar. Call (314) 727–0880 for more information.

A couple of art galleries in the area may pique your fancy. There are a number of fine galleries to explore in the St. Louis area, so don't let this small sampling give you the idea that's all there is. The **River Road Gallery** in the Swiss Village Bookstore specializes in historical and river art, and it just seems to fit the Old St. Louis feeling around here. It's located in Laclede's Landing at 707 North First Street, and it's open Monday through Friday from 10:00 A.M. to 5:00 P.M., in the winter. During the summer, owners John and Elaine Stratton keep the doors open until 9:00 P.M. and are open on Sunday from noon to 7:00 P.M.

The Laumeier Sculpture Park is located about 12 miles southwest of downtown St. Louis. The art work here is grand and huge. Artist Alexander Liberman's *The Way* is made of steel

7

cylinders intended for use as underground storage tanks. He arranged them in bent piles and welded them together. The whole thing was painted bright red. In June and July sculptors work for weeks on detailed sand castles; in winter a fire-and-ice sculpture made of giant ice blocks glows amid roaring bonfires. The ninety-six–acre park has more than sixty pieces. The wooded path hides human-size sheet metal figures by Ernest Trova. Special events—symphony, dance, ballet and theater productions—and a gallery full of indoor art are there too. A cafe and museum shop are inside, but outdoors is more fun. Take Interstate-44 to Lindbergh Boulevard, go south ½ mile, and turn right on Rott Road; the park entrance is ½ mile on the left. It is open daily from 7:00 A.M. until a half hour after sunset. Gallery hours are 10:00 A.M. to 5:00 P.M. Tuesday through Saturday; noon to 5:00 P.M. on Sunday. Admission is free. Self-guided tours are offered on audiocassettes that you can borrow from the park office. For information call (314) 821–1209.

Florissant, just north of downtown St. Louis, is so called because the first inhabitants found it a beautiful, flowering valley. It still is—but that's not all the town has to offer. Jesuit father Pierre Jean DeSmet, champion of the Indian nations, founded the **Old St. Ferdinand's Shrine.** It's now open to the public at 1, rue St. Francois (314–837–2110). The picturesque St. Stanislaus Jesuit Museum, once a self-sufficient monastery, complements the shrine; it also boasts a surprising collection of rare Greek and Latin tomes dating from 1521. The address is 700 Howdershell Road, just north of Interstate 270. The shrine is open from 1:00 to 4:00 P.M. on Sunday from April to mid-December. Call (314) 837–3525 for more information.

You should not go to St. Louis without visiting The Hill, southwest of the city, an Italian neighborhood famous for its restaurants. There is no favorite, because it depends on the type of ambiance you seek. The best bargain is probably **Cunetto's House of Pasta** at 5453 Magnolia. It's a good place to take the family, prices are very good, and the atmosphere is Continental —tablecloths, wine, no bright lights, and a full-service bar. Owner Frank Cunetto calls it gourmet Italian with good prices. His dad and uncle opened the doors more than twenty-one years ago, and it has been a popular spot ever since. Hours for lunch are Monday through Friday from 11:00 A.M. to 2:00 P.M.

Dinner is served from Monday through Thursday from 5:00 to 10:30 P.M. and on Friday and Saturday until 11:30 P.M. Call (314) 781–1135 for information.

Be sure and take the time to visit **St. Ambrose Church,** the Hill's centerpiece about four blocks from Cunetto's. It's Lombardy Romanesque and was the first acoustical plaster church in St. Louis. The columns of scagliola plaster look like marble. It is a lost art using plaster, ground gypsum, sponges, and polishing. The statues were donated by groups from different villages in Italy. Across the street is **Milo's Bocce Garden** where locals gather. When you settle in with one of the restaurant's Italian sausage sandwiches or anchovy pizzas to watch the Bocce leagues play, it sounds—and feels—as though you have crossed the Atlantic.

If you prefer to head south instead, you'll find St. Louis's own French Quarter in historic Soulard, 2 miles south of the Arch on Broadway. There's a dandy mix of period architecture and pubs, cafes, and shops for you to browse in. You can buy everything from turnips to live chickens on Saturday mornings in the busy Farmers' market in this French/Irish neighborhood, and finish off at a well-stocked spice shop. Soulard is an old brewery neighborhood where rehabilitated row houses line the streets. The Anheuser-Busch brewery is nearby and when the wind is right you can smell hops and barley cooking. Soulard also has a large collection of jazz and blues clubs. If you like the feel of this neighborhood, stay at the **Soulard Inn,** a three-story Victorian built in 1850. The Queen Anne suite on the second floor has two antiques-filled bedrooms, the third floor is the Soulard Suite, with two bedrooms done in casual country decor. The baths have claw-foot tubs. Rooms are $68, and $95 with private bath.

For information on this B&B, and many others in the state you can call **Ozark Mountain Country Reservation Service** (800) 695–1546. (Kay Cameron is especially helpful if you are touring the Ozarks and headed for Branson.)

Antiques stores line both sides of Cherokee Street for four blocks in the funky antiques district south of downtown. Prices here are very affordable, and there are dusty treasures in dark corners and beautifully restored pieces as well. You will find rare books, antique linens and lace, and glassware; and shop owners will still haggle on the price of more expensive items.

If you want to stay in the St. Louis area, but not in the city

9

itself, there is a cluster of suburban cities nearby. Many of them have bed and breakfast inns available through the **River Country Bed and Breakfast Service** at (314) 771–1993. River Country lists B&Bs throughout Missouri that can be reached only through the service. Ask for Mike Warner; she will have all the information you need, including listings in Des Peres, Ladue, and Creve Coeur.

Okay, it's easy to make jokes about a **Dog Museum,** and everyone who writes for a living has given it a doggone good try. But man's best friend deserves to be celebrated, and this canine tribute located in the 1853 Greek Revival Jarville House in St. Louis County's Queeny Park, about 18 miles west of the St. Louis riverfront, is worth a visit if you are seeking the best art of dogdom. Begin with the oil-on-mahogany portrait of the ex-Presidential pet Millie, the English springer spaniel who called the White House home for four years. See a sculpted bronze whippet, a massive wooden mastiff (once part of a carousel ride), and many works of art commissioned by breeders of show-winning dogs. Coonhounds, retrievers, and herders join Dalmatians, bloodhounds, and Afghans. Pekingese, wolfhounds, and dogs of every variety, including those of more mixed heritage, are celebrated in paintings, woodcarvings, ceramic figurines, and photographs that show them doing what dogs do—sniffing, running, licking, sleeping, or just being there. The gift shop will give you paws for thought with posters, stationery, and dozens of trinkets bearing likenesses of dogs and dog accessories (tie clasps made of tiny dog biscuits, for example).

Every Sunday afternoon the popular "Dog of the Week" program features a guest breeder, trainer, or veterinarian and a dog for demonstration. A book and videotape library allows potential dog owners to judge the merits of various breeds. In the past, well-mannered dogs were welcome to tour the gallery with their owners, but because of too many "accidents," that was stopped. The Dog Museum at 1721 South Mason Road is open from 9:00 A.M. until 5:00 P.M. Tuesday through Saturday and from noon to 5:00 P.M. on Sunday. Take Interstate 64/Highway 40 west past the Interstate 270 loop, exit on Mason Road and drive south. Watch for the signs. Admission is $3.00 for adults; $1.50 for ages sixty and up; and $1.00 for children ages five to fourteen. The program begins around 2:00 P.M. Call (314) 821–DOGS for more information.

WINE COUNTRY

Outside St. Louis on Interstate 44 west is the town of ◆ **Eureka,** which houses sixty-four antique and craft shops. Pick up a complete list of shops at the first one you spot as you come off the interstate. This town could be a one-stop, shop-till-you-drop experience, but that would be crazy, because you are now heading into an antiques-hunter's heaven.

Between Eureka and the town of Pacific is a place to slow down, be quiet, and meditate. **The Black Madonna of Czestochowa Shrine and Grottos,** operated by the Franciscan Missionary Brothers, is located there. Whether your interest is historical or spiritual, don't miss this one. Take a guided tour or just have lunch in the large picnic pavilion. Call (314) 938–5361 for information.

Midwesterners seem to have a deeply rooted preference for smoked flavor, probably from all those nights our ancestors spent around a campfire; who can resist a terrific country ham, hickory-smoked bacon, or a tender slab of ribs? You won't have to if you pay a visit to the **Smoke House Market** at 16806 Chesterfield Airport Road in Chesterfield (314–532–3314). Everything is smoked the natural way, with no preservatives and real hickory smoke. Smoked pork chops, lamb chops, Cajun sausage, along with the ribs and bacon, are available in the shop. Owners Thom and Jane Sehnert planned it that way, and Jane's got the background for it; her folks had owned the business since 1952.

The Sehnerts branched out recently and opened **Annie Gunn's** next door, a grill with an Irish theme, complete with Irish potato soup and a menu of unusual sandwiches and meat from the smokehouse. The most popular is the Boursin burger covered with highly spiced garlic and herb cheese. And there is the braunschweiger sandwich, the Cajun sausage sandwich, fabulous smoked lamb chops, ribs, Reubens, French dips. . .and the list goes on.

To find the smokehouse, follow your nose, or if your sniffer isn't highly trained, follow Highway 40 to the Airport Road exit and double back; it's about 30 miles west of St. Louis.

Highway 100 along the Missouri River is a beautiful drive any time of year, because of the white sycamores marking the river's course; in autumn it's spectacular. The Missouri River Valley deserves plenty of time; there's a lot to see and experience.

St. Albans is an anachronism, a tiny, planned community founded in the 1930s by the Johnson Shoe Company family. Five thousand acres of gorgeous rolling hills and meadows reminded Mr. Johnson of an area in England known as St. Albans, and he made it into a working farm. It is some 30 miles west of the city limits of St. Louis on Highway 100, an easy day trip and a destination not to be missed.

Aficionados of French cuisine may remember Le Bistro in the town of Chesterfield. Restaurateurs Gilbert and Simone Andujar closed that place when highway work made it difficult to reach, but take heart. Simone spotted the lovely gardens of St. Albans and chose the location for a new restaurant, **Malmaison** (314–458–0131). (Those whose French is a bit tenuous may wonder if the name means "bad house," and it would if it were two words. Native Frenchwoman Simone says that the lovely flowers reminded her of the garden where Josephine met Napoleon in her homeland, a garden named Malmaison.) The dining experience here is superb, as is the food; it's a favorite retreat for St. Louisians. Hours are Wednesday through Sunday, 11:30 A.M. to 2:30 P.M., for lunch, and 5:00 to 9:30 P.M. for dinner (10:00 P.M. on Saturday).

Hard-core bicyclists love the St. Albans region. It is full of challenging hills near the Missouri River and great views.

❿**Hunter's Hollow Inn and Restaurant** (314–742–2279) in Labadie at Washington and Front streets is a wonderful side trip for a French country lunch or dinner—or a bit of relaxation—at the Decoy Lounge. Take your pick: the dining room offers classic French country cuisine—featuring wild game, pheasant and duck, as well as lamb, veal and beef—by chef Claude Courtoisier or Missouri hickory-smoked specialties. B&B facilities are also available. Lunch is served from 11:00 A.M. until 2:00 P.M., and dinner is from 5:30 until 9:00 P.M. on Tuesday, Wednesday, and Thursday. On Friday and Saturday lunch is from 11:00 A.M. to 2:00 P.M., and dinner is from 5:30 to 10:00 P.M. Sunday hours are noon to 8:00 P.M. Hunter's Hollow is also listed with the River Country Bed & Breakfast Service. Call (314) 771–1993 for information.

This is Missouri's Rhineland, the wine growing region. Both

Attractions in Washington and Hermann

oenophiles (wine connoisseurs) and devotees of wine coolers will enjoy tasting what the state has to offer. There are two schools of thought about Missouri wines: Some say that because a majority of the grapes grown here are European vines on wild grape or Concord root stock (and some self-rooted French hybrids), the wines will be different from California or French wines. Others, purists to be sure (and the Mt. Pleasant Winery falls into this category), say that they will hold Missouri's best wines against California wines in a blind tasting any day and challenge connoisseurs to single them out. They have done so for *Les Amis du Vin,* or Friends of Wine, a wine tasting club. Whether you are a member of Les Amis du Vin or just a wine lover, you will notice that the wines of Missouri are as varied as the vintners who make them, so don't judge Missouri wines by the first place you stop.

The Frene Creek white wines rival those of the Rhine River Valley. Pop wine drinkers will love Missouri's blends of fruit wines. The peach wine made by Stone Hill and the cherry wine by Hermannhoff are a treat over ice in the hot summer months.

Washington Landing was first settled in the early 1800s. Lewis and Clark passed through the site of the future town of Washington in search of the Northwest Passage, and pronounced it promising because of its excellent boat-landing site. Located in the curve where the great river reaches the most southern point in its course, Washington is still a good place to stop when headed west.

The old 1888 waterworks building on Lafayette Street, down on the riverbank across the railroad track, now houses the **Progue Sculpture Studio.** Artist Larry Progue, chairman of the art department at East Central College in Union, shows modern sculpture in stainless steel, aluminum, brass, and tin. Larry describes himself as an "abstract expressionist direct metal sculptor." His new studio garden, at 5631 Steutermann Road, displays twenty major pieces of abstract stainless steel art. Go to the highway 47/100 intersection, then ½ mile south on Highway 47. Call Larry at (314) 239–0668 for information.

Speaking of artists, don't miss the **Gary R. Lucy Gallery** at Main and Elm streets. You may recognize Gary's work if you've picked up a Southwestern Bell telephone book from recent years; his work has graced the cover.

Gary is an extremely thorough young man. To get just the

right feeling in his series of Missouri River paintings, the artist took his boat as far upriver as was navigable, to Ft. Benton, Montana, and explored interesting areas from there back to Washington. No wonder his paintings ring true. Call (314) 239–6337 for information.

Just across Front Street and down a bit from Progue's at Lafayette is **Linen & Lace.** This shop, full of lovely European-style lace curtains, bedcovers, and tablecloths, occupies a Federal-style building beside the river. Owner Sunny Drewell's business has done so well that she closed the Zechariah Foss Bed and Breakfast upstairs and moved Linen & Lace into the entire building. The mail-order catalog is a charmer, photographed right here in the house. If you can't make it to Washington (much less to Europe) in person, call (800) 332–LACE to get the Linen & Lace catalog.

Right across the street you can spend a night steeped in history. The 1837 **Washington House Inn** first served as an inn; it has since put in its time as a general store, riverboat captain's house, fish market, speakeasy, restaurant, and apartment house. Now it has come full circle, offering nineteenth-century lodging combined with contemporary comforts. All rooms feature views of the Missouri River, queen-size canopy beds, private baths, and a fine breakfast. Stenciled walls and period furniture, mostly from the Missouri Valley area, add to the ambience. Take time to unwind and watch the river traffic and trains from the balcony or terrace. (If you find the sound of night trains romantic, the tracks are just across the street.) Hostess Cathy Davis has recently completed a new Victorian room with a double bed. It costs $65 a night; other rooms are $75.

Smoking is prohibited due to the historic nature of the building and its furnishings. For more information call (314) 239–2417). Downstairs is a tiny shop called . . . ❧ **not just Cut and Dried,** owned by Carolyn McGettigan, who has a wonderful selection of coffees, herbs, teas, and dried bouquets. Sit down and have a steaming cup of cinnamon coffee with Carolyn and she will make scouting Washington easier (314) 239–9084.

Char-Tony's, 116 West Front Street, is an Italian restaurant with a great variety of pasta dishes. Of course, there is chicken, veal, and really good steaks, too. Tony Tumminello grew up on The Hill in St. Louis, and he and his fiancee, Charleen Duncan

15

and her son Don Duncan have taken this beautiful riverfront spot and created a lovely place to dine. A fountain bubbles inside, the big bay window in front overlooks the river as does the outdoor garden on the side. They have an extensive wine list featuring Missouri wines as well as the usual California choices. There is a full bar. This is the place for fine dining in a casual atmosphere. Prices range from $6.95 to $14.95. Call (314) 239–2111 for information.

Only fifty years or so after Meriwether Lewis, his dog Scannon, and his partner William Clark passed by this likely town site, Bernard Weise built his home and tobacco store here on Front Street.

Now that location holds **The American Bounty Restaurant,** and although the magnificent view is still one of soft moonlight reflecting on the river flowing outside, inside white tablecloths await lovers of fine food and wine. Owner Dan Hacker and chef Brian Manhardt have restored this 104–year-old building at 430 West Front Street to its original splendor. The food is what they call "New Age American," or American food with a flair. Examples include encrusted chicken rolled in hash-browned potatoes, nine-way pasta, and red baby-clam sauce. The green-apple cobbler is a specialty, but it takes a half hour to prepare so order it with dinner to ensure it arrives hot when you are ready for it. Lunch is served from 11:30 A.M. until 2:00 P.M., and you can eat on the patio when the weather is nice. Dinner is served from 5:30 until 9:00 P.M. Wednesday and Thursday, until 10:00 P.M. on Friday and Saturday, and until 8:00 P.M. Sunday. Seating outside in the wine garden creates a romantic mood, and the wine list features both California and Missouri wines.

You are deep into wine country here, and there is no shortage of wineries along the valley. Most offer tastings; you can choose the ones most convenient for your schedule and location. Some offer unusual wines and are well worth the effort to search out.

One of the newest wineries in the Missouri Valley region, **Robller Vineyard** is in a quaint country setting featuring a view of the area's rolling hills. Turn south on the quarry road just east of New Haven, turn right at the first gravel road, and proceed ⅛ of a mile to the winery. Wine makers Robert and Lois Mueller grow vidal, seyval, norton, and steuben grapes for a sweet, or semisweet wine. Wine tastings here have cheese and sausage to complement the wines. In fact, they whip up great Cajun and barbecue dinners by appointment for groups. The winery is open March through December and weekends in January and February from 10:00 A.M. until dark. (It opens at noon on Sunday.) Call (314) 237–3986 for information.

The town of New Haven sits quietly on the river, and there are a number of places worth looking for downtown. Carol Hebbler has a shop and bed and breakfast at the **One Twenty-five Front Street Inn,** (314) 237–3534. The first floor holds **Collections Old and New,** a shop filled with flowers, antiques, crafts, and collectibles of all sorts. Above the shop is an apartment filled with fine antiques. A bottle of wine and fresh flowers await guests. The apartment (which will sleep four) has a living room, working kitchen, dining room, and private bath, as well as a bedroom suite with a sitting room where you can curl up in an antique swing and watch the river flow by. The rooms are huge; the bedroom has a queen-size bed, and it is $85 including a Continental breakfast in the morning. There is also cable television, a VCR, and a stereo hidden among the antiques.

◆ **Bias Vineyards & Winery** in picture-postcard Berger (pronounced *BER-jer,* population 214) lies on Highway B just off Highway 100. The setting sun at Berger reflects on the river and rugged limestone bluffs; it throws long shadows across the tilled bottomland along the river. Follow the signs to a wooded hillside. As you start up the hill, there is a railroad crossing at the foot of the rise to the vineyards. (It could be dangerous when you leave; a mirror hangs in a tree to give drivers a view of the tracks, so proceed slowly.)

Owners are Jim and Norma Bias. Jim was a TWA captain based in St. Louis. They bought the land fifteen years ago when they were looking for a country spot within commuting distance to St. Louis's Lambert Field. It came with seven acres of vines. "We had to do something with the grapes," says Norma, so they invested in a roomful of stainless-steel tanks and went into the wine business. One thing led to another, and soon Norma was in the banquet business.

Saturday night buffet dinners are scheduled on the vineyard grounds from April to December; reservations are a must. Gourmet meals are served along with Bias wines. Winter is less hectic and the Biases invite cross-country skiing on their property when the snow comes. They offer vine cuttings during the January pruning season for creating wreaths or smoking meats. Call (314) 834–5475 for more information. Winery hours are 10:00 A.M. to 6:00 P.M., Monday through Saturday, and from 11:00 A.M. until 6:00 P.M. on Sunday.

Next on the road is Hermann. To orient yourself, begin at the Hermann Visitors' Information Center at 306 Market Street. Jack Haney, the guy with the moustache and Bavarian hat, also runs Whiskey Jack's Museum of Prohibition-era memorabilia. He will tell you all about Hermann. Founded in 1836 by members of the German Settlement Society of Philadelphia, it was intended as a self-supporting refuge for German heritage and traditions, a sort of "second fatherland."

George Bayer, who had immigrated in 1830, selected a site in Missouri that resembled his home in the Rhine Valley in terms of climate, soil, and richness of wild grapevines. Bayer and the other German immigrants dreamed of building one of the largest cities in the United States in the Frene Creek Valley.

The dream quickly attracted a variety of professionals, artisans, and laborers who began the task of building the city of their dreams. It never did become that giant metropolis of the immigrants' dreams; now it is a city of festivals. There is Maifest, Wurstfest, and Octoberfest, each drawing thousands of folks from all over. Amtrak helps to alleviate traffic on festival weekends.

In winter and on non-festival weekends, Hermann is just what it looks like—a quaint German town, quiet, and filled with B&Bs, from the huge White House Hotel to the tiny Seven Sisters Bed and Breakfast Cottage. You'll find galleries, shops, and brick homes snugged right up to the street, European-style. During the festivals, though, it becomes crowded and noisy, as busy as Bayer's dream city. Portable toilets appear on street corners, and the revelry spills from wineries downtown. If you want to be off the beaten path around here, you should aim at a weekday in the off-season. Then a traveler has this sleepy hamlet all to himself.

The **Stone Hill Winery** on Stone Hill Highway just off Twelfth Street (314–386–2221) is owned by Jim and Betty Held. The world-renowned cellars are carved into the hillside, and there's a breathtaking view of the town. **Vintage 1847 Restaurant** shares the picturesque hilltop location; a huge window at one end of the restored carriage house looks out on Missouri's blue hills. Visit the restaurant's wine cellar to choose the evening's libation, and do scrutinize the menu carefully—there's a cheesecake to die for. (Take home the *Vintage 1847 Cookbook;* it's a great gift idea.)

Once in town be sure to see the ◆**Hermannhoff Winery Festhalle,** the world's largest wine hall, where you can dance to live German bands every Saturday and Sunday, starting at noon. There is no entrance fee. Enjoy a festival German dinner or a *brat mit krauts* on a bun.

There are so many great little antiques and craft shops that it would be impossible to list them all and of course there are many B&Bs in Hermann. Among them is ◆**Birk's Gasthaus,** Elmer and Gloria Birk's place at 700 Goethe Street (314–486–3143). This Victorian mansion was built by the owner of the third-largest winery in the world and is furnished in period antiques, including some 6–foot-long tubs with gold eagle-claw feet, brass beds, and 10-foot-tall doors with transoms. Birk's offers Mansion Mystery Weekends the first two full weekends of every month. These are sold out months in advance. The Birks write new theme mysteries each month, and the action happens in the gasthaus among the guests, with Showboat Community Theater members as characters—the Halloween mystery stars Frankenstein, for example.

Lovers of Christmas—the old-fashioned kind—will love **Pelze Nichol Haus Bed and Breakfast,** 109 East Broadway (314–486–3886). The home dates from 1845 to 1850 and is on the Historic Register; it's just across from the Visitors' Center off Market Street. Here Jack and Chris Cady have created a Christmas fantasy that lasts year-round. This isn't your commercial red-and-green image, though. It's all natural, old-style German, with subdued colors and plenty of Pelze Nichols to remind you of the past.

Who is Pelze Nichol, you say? The name means Furry Nicolas, the German Santa—or his helper. (Perhaps you recognize him as Belznickle, instead.)

Stay in one of three rooms—the Christmas Room, the Tannenbaum Room, or the Christmas Morning Cottage—each with its own tree made by Chris herself, and each with a private bath. Don't miss the Santa Shop, also on the premises. After spending time in this delightful place, you'll want to take home a Pelze Nichol of your own; Chris makes all style and sizes.

One of the last ferries in the state is the *Roy J* across the Gasconade River at Fredericksburg, population ten, last census. Find Highway J, 15 miles southwest of Hermann. The fare is $2.00 one way or $3.00 round trip. The ferry travels from sunrise to sunset. Call Albert Deppe (314) 294–7203 for more information.

River's Edge Restaurant is right there, too. Steve and Linda Simon serve Cajun food at the riverbank location Wednesday through Sunday. Open at noon each day, the restaurant closes at 8:30 P.M. Monday through Thursday, 10:00 P.M. on Friday and Saturday, and 8:00 P.M. on Sunday. Call (314) 294–7207 for more information.

The small village of Westphalia, south on Highway 63, perches like a lighthouse on the hill. There is only one street, with homes built right up to the sidewalk as they are in Hermann. Everything is spic-and-span and a pleasure to the eye—*das ist gut.*

The **Westphalia Inn** (314–455–9991) offers family-style meals—mashed potatoes and gravy, green beans, and an unbeatable fried chicken dinner. It is nothing fancy, just good old "comfort food" at reasonable rates. Tom and Melody Buersmeyer feed folks from 5:00 to 8:00 P.M. Thursday through Saturday and Sunday from noon until 8:00 P.M.

There is also a bed and breakfast in a distinctive home that connects to the post office, with a private suite and plenty of room for extra guests. Rates are $45 to $50; make reservations through the River Country Bed and Breakfast (314–965–4328).

Zeke's Country Wood Products is on Highway E in Rich Fountain. In this old bank building, Zeke makes reproduction furniture using the same methods used in the original models, square nails and all. He also refinishes antiques. He and his family moved here from St. Louis and bought the 120-year-old stone house that they are in the process of restoring. His hours are Thursday through Sunday from 10:00 A.M. until 5:00 P.M. Stop by and see his work. Call (314) 744–5424 for information.

On the east side of Highway 63 at Vienna, the ◆**Americana Antique, Art and Curio Shop** is a house and garage and several outbuildings (including a huge barn), all filled to the ceiling with what owner John Viessman calls "stuff." Everything you can imagine, from old army uniforms to a disassembled log cabin he is rebuilding—to hold some more stuff. Stuff like time-card racks out of an old factory, pictures, ancient trunks, and dolls. Not just little stuff, but big stuff, like a walnut wardrobe that measures 6 feet wide and 9 feet tall. But his real passion is books, especially books about Missouri history, and there are over 30,000 books in the house, two deep in floor-to-ceiling shelves running through what was once the living room. Volumes on the Civil War, Jewish folklore, and the black experience in America are crammed together in some kind of order ("it's a constant struggle," he says) along with old Dick and Jane books and McGufefy *Readers* and an 1824 textbook. Books are everywhere among the other stuff, too. There is a whole wall of *Life* magazines set up by year so that people can find their birthday issue. John still goes to auctions and sales and carts more stuff home, and he has been doing this for over twenty years. He and his wife Kelley McCall have a studio there, too—Kelley is a photographer, and John paints. John seems to know everyone for miles around Vienna. John is around most weekends, when he isn't at a sale, and the shop is open by chance or by appointment. There's a large sign in the front yard announcing OPEN or CLOSED so you can just drive by and check it out (314–422–3505).

Vienna has only about 600 residents, but what an interesting bunch of folks they are! There's even a recording studio in town that people from Nashville come to use. The Old Jail Museum is three blocks east on Highway 42, and you can visit it from 2:00 until 4:00 P.M. on Sunday in the summertime. Two miles down the Ball Park Road is one of the nine swinging bridges left in the state. The circa 1855 Latham Log House has been restored; it is near the Old Jail Museum.

Kathy and Tom Corey returned home to Maries County after thirty years and built their dream home in the rock-strewn hills above the Gasconade River. They decided to share it and a country inn was born. The name, **rock eddy bluff** comes from the location of the inn. It sits atop a rugged limestone bluff overlooking the river. Here the water curves and quickens over a shoal, then calms into a deeper pool set against the bluffs. A series of large boulders rises above the water (Thox rock is the largest), which gave this section of the river the name rock eddy. The inn offers private access to the Gasconade River, and canoes are available. You can see 10 miles across the river valley between Vienna and

Dixon from here. It is more a country retreat than a B&B. There's hiking and a horse-drawn Amish spring wagon. Scenic Clifty Creek has worn a natural arch through the bluff. The inn's upper story boasts a pretty view of the river; it offers two bedrooms which share a sitting room and bath. A cottage ½ mile from the house overlooks the river and offers a full kitchen and three bedrooms that will sleep eight persons comfortably. A great place to take the family. Halfway to the river in a grove of maples, Tom is completing a primitive cabin that will be a step back in time. It will have no electricity and an old-fashioned ice box and kerosene lamps. To reach rock eddy bluff, take Highway 63 through Vienna, two miles out of Vienna turn on Highway 28. The price is $59 with breakfast. There is no charge for canoes or horse-and-buggy rides. The cottage costs $97 plus $10 for each extra person. It is worth every penny. You will see nesting bald eagles that have been there for years and a great blue heron rookery with about fifty nests in the clutch of trees. For more information call (314) 759–6081.

About four miles north of Vienna on the west side of Highway 63, **The Richard Blancher Studio** houses some large, very large, works. There is a 31,000-pound piece of stone sculpture, and a 10-foot-by-30-foot painting. This artist doesn't do anything half-way. This high ground is so picturesque overlooking the four lakes nearby, that Richard is opening a country inn here in late 1996. The entrance to the studio is between two of the lakes—which, he mentions, are well-stocked—and his hours are from "about 7:00 A.M. until about dark," he says. He can be reached at (314) 422–6119.

Next up on Highway 63 where it intersects with 14th Street (take exit 186 off Interstate 44) is Rolla. Here the famous Rolla School of Mines is located. If you are interested in mines or minerals, it's worth your while to see the museum. Be sure to take the time to see **Missouri's Stonehenge,** a half-scale version of the English one built 4,000 years ago. Missouri's version was built by the school's specialists in the fields of mining engineering, rock mechanics, explosives research, civil engineering, and computer science. It was built to honor the techno-nerds of long ago who built theirs to pinpoint the solstices and changing seasons with moonlight and sunlight falling through precisely positioned stones. The new Stonehenge, however, was built of 160 tons of granite, shaped by cutting torches and high-pressure water jets and aligned by computer. It also includes an "analemma" solar calendar used by the Anasazi Indians in the American Southwest more than 1,000 years ago and a Polaris window for sighting the North Star. It was dedicated in 1984 on the summer solstice. A member of the Society of Druids offered ancient incantations over this blend of the ancient and ultramodern.

If you like Cajun food and all those rocks have made you hungry, don't miss **Papa Meaux Restaurant.** This home-style spot is casual, as you'd expect, and full of the best kind of authentic, spicy Cajun food you might not. Andouille sausage, étouffée, jambalaya, gumbo, or bread pudding to die for—whatever your pleasure, Papa will provide. You will find this crawfish heaven at 1205 Kingshighway. Hours are 11:00 A.M. to 10:00 P.M. Tuesday through Saturday and 11:00 A.M. to 2:00 P.M. on Sunday —Papa rests on Monday. Call (314) 368–5586 for information.

There's a lot happening in St. James on Highway 68 east of Rolla, if you are an oenophile (that's a wine lover, remember?). Stop by **St. James Winery,** at 540 Sidney Street (314–265–7912) or visit **Heinrichshaus Vineyards and Winery,** a family-owned winery specializing in dry wines, including vidal blanc and chambourcin. Heinrich and Lois Grohe are the owners and wine masters. Heinrich is from southern Germany, and their daughter Peggy went to school in Switzerland, where she studied wine making. The winery offers fresh grapes in season, Missouri cheeses and sausages, hand-thrown pottery, and original watercolors and prints by Missouri artists. Now this is a full-service winery—wine and cheese, a clay carafe, and original art to enjoy while you picnic on the winery grounds. Spring and fall bring festivals and bike tours to the winery. Call (314) 265–5000 for a calendar of events and directions or watch for signs; this is on a rural route. A loaf of bread, a jug of wine, and a picnic! Hours are 9:00 A.M. to 6:00 P.M. every day but Wednesday and holidays.

◆ **Ferrigno's Winery and B&B** is an interesting place to spend some time in the St. James area. Wine makers Dick and Susan Ferrigno grow seven varieties of French hybrid grapes such as the chambourcin, a red grape, and the seyval white grape. They now have fourteen acres in vines and make nine wines ranging from very dry to semisweet. Dick's favorite wines are made from the Cynthiana, which is a red grape, and seyval grapes. Recent DNA testing proved what many wine makers had suspected for some years—that the Cynthiana and the Norton are the same grape. These wines are dry with a definite oak flavor. You may peer through glass to watch the wine making process at the winery or wander in the surrounding vineyards. Susan serves dinner in the wine pavilion to private groups, and there is always wine, sausage and other items available for picnics on the grounds.

The vineyard also houses a B&B. The renovated dairy barn, now the winery, has a room above it called the Loft. A nearby cottage has two suites and guests have the run of the wooded forty acres. Take Interstate 44 to the St. James exit, go 200 feet to Highway B, turn right and go 4½ miles to Ferrigno's, which is on the left. There's good fishing and hiking and the vineyard separates the Ferrigno's home from the guest cottage. Breakfast is served in their kitchen or often in the wine garden. Prices range from $69 to $89 and include a bottle of wine of your choice and a full breakfast. Winery hours are Monday through Saturday from 10:00 A.M. to 6:00 P.M. every day but Sunday, which is noon to 6:00 P.M. Call (314) 265–8050 for reservations.

Deep underground in the unchanging atmosphere beloved by spelunkers, the longest underground river flows silently through ❖ **Onondaga Cave** in the Daniel Boone State Park near Leasburg on Interstate 44 east of St. James. This is a place of superlatives: Massive stalagmites rise like peaks from the floor of the Big Room, the largest cave living room in the world. In Daniel Boone's Room the abundance of cave formations is enough to make you shake your head in amazement. Old Dan himself discovered the place in 1798—or rather, he was the first white man to do so. Native Americans had used the area as a hunting sanctuary from earliest times.

Organizers of the St. Louis World's Fair in 1904 encouraged the cave's owners to open it to the public—it was a great hit, as visitors came first by railroad and then by surrey and wagon to explore the wonders.

Bourbon, off Interstate 44, was once a whiskey stop on the railroad—could you tell from the name? Now it's the home of **Meramec Farm Stays,** modeled after the Australian incarnation of the bed and breakfast experience. In the same family since 1811, and now into its fifth generation, this family farm has earned the Missouri Century Farm sign awarded by the University of Missouri to farms that have been in the same family for at least one hundred years.

This is a real working farm, with critters and all—kids who don't have a grandma in the country will enjoy petting the horses, feeding the ducks, or playing in a real old-fashioned hayloft.

It's great for adults, too. If you want to help out around the farm, you may. If not, just enjoy the 1½-mile trail that adjoins the highest bluffs on the Meramec River. Take a dip in a swimming hole, picnic on a gravel bar, or enjoy canoeing on a section of the Meramec that doesn't require a class-five rapids expert.

The price is still $50 with breakfast (an event which, like the other meals served on the farm, features fresh-baked breads, farm-raised fruits, vegetables, and meats), or $65 for two with dinner. The 470-acre farm is just an hour's drive from St. Louis. It lies on a bend in the Meramec River near the Vilander Bluffs. A conveniently located five-acre gravel bar is there for people who want to fish and swim. Tubing and canoeing are some of the favorite activities. There is also a guest cabin built from the farm's own cedars. The two bedrooms and loft can accommodate eight people. It has a full kitchen and screened porch—and a great view. The cabin is $50 for two (with breakfast) plus $10 for each child under twelve or plus $15 each for teens. (Slightly more with Saturday dinner.) Something new has been added: Now you can bring your horse with you and Meramec Farms will provide bed and breakfast service for that member of your family, too. Trail rides are two- or three-hour private half-day rides following a hearty breakfast. The ride takes you on a tour of the farm from the river fields to the highest hilltop view. An old family cemetery is on the trail. For the private ride, the first rider is $25, and each additional rider is $10. Children under twelve are half price.

Carol Springer asks that you call ahead for reservations and directions. It is a working farm, and drop-ins tend to arrive at just the wrong time; but Carol and her husband David Curtis have been juggling it all for eleven years now, so they must be doing something right. For reservations call Carol Springer, HCR 1, Box 50, Bourbon, MO 65441 or phone or fax (314) 732–4765.

Wild Flower Inn near Sullivan (314–468–7975) is owned by Mary Lou and Jerry Hubble. The lovely county inn on forty-two acres is just 2 miles off Interstate 44. The four guest rooms all have private baths and televisions. There is a gathering room, and in the summer, guests can eat outside on the big front porch. Guests have access to the kitchen to make coffee any time, and a big country breakfast is served at the hour of your choice. What a choice, too: Belgian waffles, soufflés, quiches—this couple loves to cook—blueberry pancakes fresh in season, and they will custom cook for people with dietary needs. Everything is homemade and "you don't go away hungry" Jerry says. It could be a private getaway during the week, because most guests come on weekends. You even have your own key. The inn was built for a B&B; it's all new but looks like an old mill. Rooms upstairs cost from $70 to $75. The Honeymoon suite has queen-size beds and a large European-style bath, so you can feel like a country gentleman/woman. It's a quiet adult getaway place.

There's an antiques mall in Sullivan; Mary Lou will direct you there. The town has a lot of mom-and-pop restaurants. It's lovely in the fall. Meramec river is nearby for floaters.

◆**Meramec State Park Lodge** at Sullivan, east on Interstate 44, is an excellent spot for canoeing and exploring, though it is often crowded on summer weekends. Meramec State Park on the scenic Meramec River winds through the rough, timbered hills just east of Little Bourbon.

Missouri is known as the cave state, with more known caves than any other state—5,200 counted so far. There are some twenty-two within the park. One, Fisher Cave, is open for guided tours; others are protected as habitat for an endangered bat species. (You didn't really want to go in that badly, did you?)

The folks at Stanton, farther east on Interstate 44, argue with the people of St. Joseph, who say Jesse James died there. Stanton proponents believe that the murder of Thomas Howard on April 3, 1882, was a clever plot to deceive investigators and authorities—with the backing of then Governor of Missouri, Thomas T. Crittendon! The ◆**Jesse James Wax Museum** tells the story of James's life in 1882, the mechanics of his incredible escape from justice, and the look-alike outlaw killed by Robert Ford.

Skeptical? Well, that's the true Show Me attitude. Take your pick. Believe that Jesse died in 1951, just three weeks shy of his 104th birthday, or that he was gunned down by his cousin more than a hundred years ago. Admission to the museum is $3.00 for adults; seniors and military $2.00; and children $1.00.

Jesse was a member of Quantrill's Raiders, who captured a gunpowder mill and used the caverns as hideouts; beneath

Stanton's rolling hills lies a complex of caves and finely colored mineral formations, as rare as they are beautiful. The nearby Meramec Caverns have guided tours, restaurants, and lodging.

WILD LANDS

South from St. Louis you have the choice of Interstate 55 or old Highway 61. (You can also take Interstate 270 if you want to bypass the city entirely.) However you get there, don't miss the museum and displays at ✦**Mastodon State Park** near Imperial; the kids will love it and so will you.

Did you know that woolly mammoths and mastodons roamed these Missouri hills just a few short millennia ago? This area contained mineral springs, which made for swampy conditions but great preservation conditions. Large mammals became trapped in the mineral-rich mud, which preserved their remains perfectly as the mud hardened to stone. You can still see the **Kimmswick Bone Bed**, which is one of the most extensive Pleistocene beds in the country and of worldwide interest to archaeologists and paleontologists. Explore the Visitors' Center, too. It offers a life-size replica of a mastodon skeleton, Clovis points, and other remnants of early human occupation. Mastodon State Park (314–464–2976) is south on Highway 55 at 1551 Seckman Road, Imperial.

Now aim just south for the town of Kimmswick, laid out in 1859 by a German named Theodore Kimm.

In the early 1880s, Kimmswick's beautiful Montesano Park attracted people from St. Louis by excursion boat. Riverboats and railroads stopped here. But the horseless carriage changed the destiny of Kimmswick; the new highway system bypassed the town, and left it to become a sleepy little backwater. Even the trains and boats no longer stopped to trade. But that isn't true any more. Now the Huck Finn riverboat paddles down from St. Louis on the second and fourth Wednesday of each month from May through October and docks in Kimmswick; the train may even return soon, but the town no longer worries about being overpowered by St. Louis. Its shops and restaurants are some of the best along the riverfront. One little shop—**It's A Small World Christmas Haus**—alone is worth diverting from the interstate to see. It is a year-round wonderland guaranteed to put you in the Christmas spirit even during July sunshine. Shop-keeper Ann Thuston and her daughters Peggy Bienefeld and Lynn Murphy keep the shop stocked with European Christmas miniatures.

Mary Hostetter, owner of the ◆ **Blue Owl Restaurant and Bakery,** says that Kimmswick refuses to be "gobbled up by St. Louis" and works to maintain its individuality as the "town that time forgot." Mary invites you to sit in front of a cheery fireplace and try a few of her specialties.

The building was erected in 1900 and called Ma Green's Tavern until the 1950s. It was restored in the 1970s and now has warm wood floors that are charmingly out of level and lace curtains in the windows. Railroad car siding covers the walls, and waitresses dressed in long pinafores serve lunch on delicate blue-and-white china. Mary recently added Miss Mary's veranda, a Victorian veranda, for outdoor dining. A new dining room just opened, too, so now there are five dining rooms. There is live German music with Austrian Paul Knopf on the accordion. Parking is available in the restaurant's lot.

The Blue Owl (314–464–3128) is open year-round Tuesday through Friday 10:00 A.M. to 3:00 P.M. and Saturday and Sunday from 10:00 A.M. to 5:00 P.M. From country breakfasts and home-made soups (the Canadian cheese soup is marvelous) on week-days to the wonderful Sunday special of homemade chicken and dumplings, Mary will try to fill you up. If you happen to see the pastry case as you come in the door, you won't allow that to happen until coffee and dessert. Take a good look at the temple of temptation: Lemon dobosh has eight layers of lemon cake with filling between each and whipped cream on top. There's an Italian cream cake, Irish apple cake, red velvet cake, and the favorite Death By Chocolate. The new Levee High Apple Pie was created to celebrate the great flood of '93 when the river crested at 39.9 feet against the 40–foot levee. There is outdoor dining May through October and a live German band.

Walk around Kimmswick; there is a lot to see here, from historic homes and businesses to some fine little restaurants, twenty-two shops, so far, and still growing. And do stop by **Kimmswick Pottery.** Artist Chris Ferbet creates hand-thrown pieces, some made from native red clay, which she digs herself. She also carries an international assortment of hand-crafted art. You can watch her working at the pottery wheel or browse around the shop.

The Old House, built in 1770, now stands at Second and Elm streets. The second story and wing were added in 1831. When you see the size of the house, it's hard to believe that it was moved from the town of Beck in 1973 to save it from demolition. Inside are several rooms, two of which have massive brick fireplaces to warm the traveler and food perfect for the atmosphere.

There is a new bed and breakfast in town, too. Shirley Berving's **Kimmswick Corner Bed and Breakfast** at the corner of Front and Market streets is upstairs over the Kimmswick Corner gift shop. The two newly refurbished rooms, with shared bath, cost $60 a night. Period wallpaper and antique furniture draw you back to the time when the original owners lived above the shop. You can call (314) 464–2028 and make reservations through the shop.

Swing southwest on Highway 67 at Crystal City to the city of Bonne Terre, a year-round resort, as interesting in December in the middle of a blizzard as it is in the heat of a 100° summer day. There isn't all that much to see—above ground, that is. But if you choose Mansion Hill as your first stop and meet owners Doug and Cathy Georgan, the town will come alive for you. In this setting it would have to; the mansion occupies the highest point in Bonne Terre, on 132 acres of timber in the Ozark foothills. Each room has its own view of the estate (which has a 45–mile view of the surrounding area). Four huge fireplaces warm the great rooms.

The 1909 mansion was built by the lead-mining baron responsible for ◆**Bonne Terre Mines** (the world's largest man-made caverns), which honeycomb the earth under the city. Hand-dug with pick and shovel, the mines are now flooded. They are the pride of the Georgans, who also own West End Diving in St. Louis. The mines can be explored two ways in any weather: by scuba diving, as do hundreds of divers who make the trek to Bonne Terre winter and summer, or by walking along the above-water trails.

Your first view of the mine is breathtaking; under the crystal clear water, illuminated from above by electric lights, divers can see all the remnants of the mining days, including ore carts, elevator shafts, buildings—even tools and drills left when the mine was abandoned in 1961. No less a personage than Jacques Cousteau was a guest at the mansion and filmed a dive here. Rooms at the mansion range from $135 to $165 and are worth every penny—the place is gorgeous.

From the entrance to the mines, turn right on Park Street and go to Allen Street. Follow it until you see the old St. Joe Lead Company Headquarters on the right and the 1909 depot on the left. The depot is built in the Queen Anne and Stick architectural styles and is on the National Historic Register. The English-style phone booth outside, a caboose, box cars and rail lamps and posts give it a 19th-century flair. Inside the depot, the **Whistle Stop Saloon** is filled with train memorabilia. The second and third floors are part of a turn-of-the-century bed and breakfast. Call (314) 358–5311 for information.

Rates are $100–$120 for two. The mansion and depot are filled almost every weekend, year-round, by clubs who travel here to scuba dive. All rooms have twin beds to accommodate the divers.

If you are hungry while in Farmington, search out **Hunt's Dairy Bar.** It was celebrated in *Midwest Living* magazine as one of the best family-owned independent drive-ins in the Midwest.

History buffs shouldn't miss the Civil War battlefield at **Fort Davidson State Historic Site** at Pilot Knob. You can still see the outlines of the hexagonal fort built in 1863 by Union forces. Flanked on three sides by high hills, the fort was vulnerable to attack from above, which must have been apparent to General Thomas Ewing. After losing seventy-five men in the Battle of Pilot Knob, he had his soldiers muffle their horses' hooves with burlap and evacuate during the night.

If you happen to be on Highway 32 headed westbound for Dillard Mill, canoeing in Salem, or hiking in the Indian Trail State Forest, you might enjoy shopping in Bixby at the ◆ **Good Ole Days Country Store.** You will notice the bright red 1946 Missouri Pacific caboose tucked against one side of the store. Owners George and Charlene Civey have modern gas pumps and Model-A vintage pumps (also painted bright red) out front, and inside is the same blend of old and new. Twenty-five cents buys a cup of coffee (on the honor system) while above your head three O-scale model trains run on a track suspended from the ceiling, complete with flashing lights and whistles. There's more to see. Antiques fill almost every available inch of space on the hardwood floors. Out back is an old log cabin turned antiques store, which also houses a collection of minerals from surrounding hills.

Bixby's general store has never closed since it was first opened in 1906 when the railroad put a siding right next to the store. The store sold everything from casket materials to plows to groceries; locals didn't have to go anywhere else (not that there was anyplace else to go anyway). The store still has a lot of convenience items and a good deli for lunch and ice cream (get a real malt) to eat in the caboose. Hours are 5:00 A.M. to 6:00 P.M. Monday through Friday and until 5:00 P.M. on Saturday. For more information call (314) 626–4868.

One of Missouri's best kept secrets is the Arcadia Valley—and its villages of Arcadia, Pilot Knob, and Ironton—where there are quite a few antiques shops. One, in Arcadia, belongs to Thomas and Margot Crowell. Old House Antiques at 105 East Walnut (314) 546–2488 is chock-full of furniture that Margot has collected. She can give you a guide to other shops in the area. The town is full of Civil War-era churches and buildings. The shop is open 10:00 A.M. to 5:00 P.M. Monday through Friday; Saturday 9:00 A.M. to 4:00 P.M., and Sunday from noon to 4:00 P.M.

Homesteader Antiques in Pilot Knob on Highway 21 and Iron County Road 103 (drive a mile, follow the signs, and drive until you see some log cabins) is where Denise Mayfield has been in business for the past four years selling furniture she refinishes by hand. One of the log cabins is her home; the other is her shop. Hours are 10:00 A.M. until 5:00 P.M. Tuesday thorough Sunday.

Lesterville may be on the map (and it is, south of Arcadia and west of Hogan on Highway 49), but it's really not a town anymore. This unincorporated village is a quiet little place nestled in wooded country that is dotted with old farms and barns. But just down the road is the Yellow Valley Forge, a combination blacksmith shop and pottery that looks more like a contemporary gallery from downtown St. Louis.

Doug Hendrickson makes elegant ironware and, in fact, does a brisk wholesale business in several states. He welcomes visitors—and spectators!—and will accept a commission if you've something special in mind.

Doug shares the shop with partner Lee Ferber, a talented potter whose Peola Valley Pottery is among the state's best. In addition to the *de rigueur* mugs and crocks, there are some terrific birdfeeders to add pizzazz to winter days. Take the old Peola road at the north end of town (it's the only way you can go) for

3 miles. Watch for circular red, green, and white signs. When you cross Yellow Valley Creek, you've found Doug and Lee's place. For details call (314) 637–2576.

Just up the road from the forge is **Wilderness Lodge** (314–637–2295), a great old-fashioned Ozarks experience that includes Black River canoe and inner tube floats and hayrides in its package. The lodge is made of logs, and the cottages are quintessential rounded Ozark-river stone, each with a fireplace.

The nearby ✦**Johnson Shut-ins** (north of Lesterville on Highway N) will surprise you with their rugged beauty, which is like terrain you'd expect to find in Maine or Colorado. These worn and convoluted forms have a story behind them; would you believe Missouri once had its own Mt. St. Helens? Prehistoric volcanic eruptions spewed tons of magma, towering clouds of ash, and acid debris, flattening vegetation and covering whole areas with newly formed igneous rock. Some 250 million years passed, and shallow inland seas encroached, covering the already ancient volcanic mountains with layers of sedimentary rock. These layers built up until they were hundreds of feet thick over the course of many millions of years.

There were more violent uplifts across the Ozarks; the seas retreated; and rain, wind, and moving water eroded the softer sedimentary rock layers, cutting the river valley ever deeper. Swirling over and between the buried igneous hills, the river scoured and carved potholes, chutes, and spectacular gorges. It is amazing that something as penetrable as water can cut the hardest stone—here's proof.

The Johnson Shut-ins are pocketed away in the scenic St. Francois Mountains; when you see them, you will understand the name. You feel isolated, hidden, shut in—but without a trace of claustrophobia. Adding to the unique nature of the area are the drought-adapted plants commonly found in the deserts of the Southwest. Scorpions and the rare eastern collared lizard (which rises to an upright position to run on its hind legs and is a treat to see) also find a home in the glades. (Never put on your boots in the morning without first shaking them out—scorpions love hiding places.)

East of the park, the Taum Sauk section of the Ozark Trail leads to **Mina Sauk Falls** (the highest falls in Missouri) and Taum

Sauk Mountain, the highest point in the state at 1,772 feet above sea level. (Okay, no snickering, this is not Colorado.)

North of the Shut-ins, through some of the prettiest hills this side of the Great Smoky Mountains, is Dillard and the ◆ **Dillard Mill State Historic Site.** Like a Currier & Ives scene beside its mill run, it is one of the state's best-preserved water-powered gristmills. This picturesque red building sits squarely at the juncture of two of the clearest-flowing Ozark streams, Huzzah and Indian creeks. The original mill machinery is still in operation, grinding away.

When you've finished with industrial history, check out the natural history. Dillard has a 1½–mile hiking trail through oak and hickory forests that ends at a pine-topped plateau.

Backtrack a bit on Highway 49 and turn east on Highway 32 to ◆ **Elephant Rocks State Park** near Graniteville. It is the first park in the state to have a trail designed especially for the visually and physically handicapped. Signs along the trail, written in braille and in regular text, describe the origin of the elephant rocks and guide visitors along a paved 1–mile path.

Elephant Rocks is one of the oddest geological formations you're likely to find in Missouri. Here monolithic boulders stand end-to-end like a train of circus elephants, dwarfing mere mortals who stand beside them. Made of billion-year-old granite, the rocks were formed during the Precambrian era when molten rock forced its way to the surface, pushing the earth's crust aside. The magma cooled and hardened slowly as this area became less volcanically active; it broke in vertical cracks, which weathered and rounded to form the huge "elephants." This weathering eventually breaks even the largest rocks down into pebbles and gravel, but not to worry: More stone elephants are in the making all the time. The pink patriarch of the pachyderm herd is Dumbo, that is 27 feet tall and 35 feet long and weighs in at a sylph-like 680 tons. Winding trails, colorful lichen and wildflowers, cool, oak-shaded grottos and a deep, clear pool just made for a summer swim add to the attractions here.

RIVER HERITAGE AREA

If you didn't head off into the wilderness back on Highway 67 at

Crystal City but stayed on Interstate 55 or Highway 61, you will now enter the River Heritage area. From river bluffs and hills to lowlands, from historic towns to waterways, the River Heritage region boasts enough destinations for several vacations. The French influence is visible everywhere you look in **Ste. Genevieve,** from the name itself to the many buildings *à la française*. The earliest records of the Missouri Territory invariably mention Ste. Genevieve and its ball-loving inhabitants!

Ste. Genevieve has been clinging to the riverbank here since the 1730s when French trappers sought valuable beaver pelts. The 5,000 people who call Sainte Gen home still celebrate Bastille Day and are justifiably proud of their French Creole-style buildings. The "Great Flood of '93" threatened the town, but it managed to stay dry with a lot of sandbagging by citizens and history-minded volunteers from all over the nation.

Many visitors to Ste. Genevieve are research scholars and genealogists from around the world. The records at the library, courthouse, and churches are the oldest in the West. St. Genevieve calls itself the oldest town west of the Mississippi (more than one Missouri town makes this claim, though) and says "all history of the West begins here."

Stop by the information center on Third Street. Many of the town's homes date to the 1700s and are preserved as historic sites and open for tours. Start with the **Ste. Genevieve Museum,** which houses one of the first bird mounts by John James Audubon himself, who did business—albeit briefly—here in the early 1800s. You'll see French-style *sabots* (wooden shoes), early songbooks, a flute belonging to Audubon's partner Rozier, and much more.

The **Bolduc House Museum,** 125 South Main Street, was built circa 1770 and moved to its current site in 1785. The two-room French colonial is one of the best examples of its type of architecture along the Mississippi. Tour guides in period costume lead visitors through the building where the yellow glow of tallow lamps dimly light the flintlock rifles above the mantel and the bison rug on the floor. Outside an herb garden, well, and orchard are inside a typical French-style palisade enclosure.

Then choose among the homes, churches, shops, and country inns dotting the town. Search out places for little treats such as Sara Menard's **Sara's Ice Cream and Antiques,** or the **D&G**

Back garden at Bolduc House Museum

Bakery and try one of their famous cream-filled crumbcakes.

You can't help but notice the **Old Brick House,** built in 1780, which faces the courthouse square, at Third and Market. It's owned by sisters Rosie and Judy Schwartz, who now run the restaurant here. Judy says the favorite entree is liver knaefly, a liver dumpling. Before you liver-haters turn up your nose, this German cook urges you to try the dish. It wouldn't be a regularly scheduled favorite if it weren't great, right? Call (314) 883–2724 for information.

Down the block at 146 South Third Street is the circa-1790 ❖**Southern Hotel** (314–883–3493). Barbara and Mike Hankins saw the old wreck, which had been abandoned since 1980, and fell in love with it. "It was such a mess," Barbara says just a bit wearily, "that finally everything quit working. We stripped it back to the walls and put in state-of-the-art electrical, plumbing, and furnace fixtures." Barbara insists they made it into a bed and breakfast to justify owning it! The hotel is full of antiques and claw-foot tubs. Meals feature fresh herbs from the garden behind the hotel and flowers from the garden fill the rooms. The garden itself is magical. An arbor leads to a wide cedar swing at the center; Mike has wired the whole area with thousands of tiny white lights. When he hits the switch at dusk the garden is a romantic fairyland. Tucked away in a corner of the garden is a great little shop with dried flowers, herbal soaps, and hand-painted goodies—don't miss it!

It has been open since 1987 with eight guest rooms, each with its own bath. Rooms cost from $80 to $125 and include such wondrous French breakfast items as strawberry soup, artichoke heart strata (a layered egg-and-bread dish), croissants, homemade lemon bread, juice and coffee.

It's an easy walk to other fine eating spots such as **Lucretia's,** a lovely old house where the rooms are filled with tables serving what is said to be the best French cuisine in town. Interesting original paintings adorn the walls and music fills the air—what more could you want?

The Steiger Haus Bed and Breakfast is at 1021 Market Street (314–883–5881 or 800–814–5881). Rob Beckerman, who is an owner and the manager, cooks and serves a full breakfast ("I do almost everything," he says), and apple crepes and cheese omelets are his specialty. This two-story house has an indoor pool, and, if you enjoy mysteries, Rob plans a murder on weekends for you to solve. Guests are always suspects, but three actors play various roles, especially dead bodies; Rob says, "we don't want to murder our guests." Rates range from $57.50 to $67.50. You can also reserve a room by calling River Country Bed and Breakfast Service, (314) 771–1993.

The information presented here only begins to touch on what is available in Ste. Gen; there's the **Sainte Genevieve Winery** at 245 Merchant Street (314–883–2800), the **Sweet Things** confection shop at 242 Market Street (314–883–7990), all manner of antiques shops and restaurants, and a whole list of B&Bs.

At Perryville, off Highway 61, is the **St. Mary of the Barrens Church,** dating to 1827. The grounds are open to walk through; be sure to visit the church's museums. This is also the National Shrine of Our Lady of the Miraculous Medal.

For more history (and fun), detour east a bit on the Great River

Road and watch for Tower Rock jutting up 85 feet out of the Mississippi. Don't miss the little German towns of Altenberg, Whittenberg, and Frohna. If you're ready to eat, ✦ **Tric's Family Restaurant** in Altenberg turns out a plentiful supply of German-style home cooking and wonderful buffets at 5:00 P.M. five nights a week. Most nights offer changing menus, but Saturday it's sauerbraten or bratwurst, and on Sunday there is a noon buffet. Homemade pies (of which coconut cream is the favorite) are plentiful, and there are always fresh fruit pies such as strawberry/rhubarb or peach. "We never, ever, use canned fruit," says Rose. The restaurant is closed Mondays.

Tric's (314–824–5387) is on Highway C and is owned by Harlin and Rose Oberndorfer. Rose can direct you to other special spots in Altenburg and Frohna including Lutheran monuments and Missouri's first Lutheran college.

Stay on Highway 61, and the next stop is Jackson; all aboard the old Iron Mountain Railroad. The oldest Protestant church west of the Mississippi, the Old McKendree Chapel (circa 1819), a national Methodist shrine, is here, and so is **Trisha's Bed and Breakfast and Tea Room and Craft Shop** at 203 Bellevue. It is the family home of Trisha and Gus Wischmann, and it is known here as "The Mueller Haus." There's a relaxed, congenial atmosphere (with respect for your privacy) and a home-cooked breakfast. A delightful resting spot—what more could you ask for? Hours are 11:00 A.M. to 4:00 P.M. Wednesday, Thursday, and Friday. Call (314) 243–7427 for more information.

The best attraction for you railroad fans is the ✦ **Iron Mountain Railway;** it's the only steam-powered tourist railroad line in the region. Sights and sounds will carry you back to the late 1800s and the early twentieth century when this was the preferred method of travel.

The "mother line" of nearly all the smaller rail lines that eventually became the historic Missouri Pacific, the Iron Mountain Railway is part of the St. Louis, Iron Mountain, and Southern Railway Company. On Saturdays you can take a round-trip ride on the train for $22, which includes dinner. Other round-trip excursions leave at various times during the day. Adults ride for $8.00; kids are half price, and those under two are free. Call (314) 243–1688 for more information.

While you're near Jackson, take a side trip to Burfordville on

Highway 34 east. The **Bollinger Mill** has been in continuous operation for more than 180 years—these people really kept their noses to the grindstone, didn't they? Located on the Whitewater River, the four-story, stone-and-brick structure shares the setting with the Burfordville Covered Bridge, one of five covered bridges remaining in the state.

Bridge building was begun in 1858 and, like much of Missouri's everyday life, was put on hold by the Civil War. The Burfordville Bridge was completed in 1868. It is a 140-foot span of incredibly long yellow poplar timbers, which grow handy to the river. It's another excellent setting for artists and photographers, not to mention history and nostalgia buffs.

Cape Girardeau is radio-and-television talk-show host Rush Limbaugh's hometown, and the city offers a self-directed (very conservative) tour (with nothing but right turns?) past the hospital where he was born, his boyhood home, high school, and barbershop where he got his first job. Then you can have lunch at his favorite hamburger joint, Wimpy's. Pick up a brochure at the Visitors' Bureau at 1707 Mount Auburn Road (800–777–0068).

You're deep in southern Missouri now, and headed for "the Cape." On Interstate 55, Cape Girardeau is the biggest city in the area, with a population of almost 35,000. But Cape Girardeau has also preserved its heritage carefully, and it's a beautiful city in spite of—and in the midst of—phenomenal growth.

Drive through the city and note the many nineteenth-century buildings. The beautiful Glenn House, circa 1880, is a good example. The old Court of Common Pleas has a lovely hilltop setting, and Cape Rock Park is a reminder of the early trading post that predated the city itself. Civil War fortifications still remain in the area. The convention and tourism bureau is at 601 North Kingshighway; if you plan to spend some time here it may pay to stop.

Although the Cape is modern and expanding too fast, all is not lost. Proceed directly down to Water Street which, as you may have guessed by the name, is along the mighty Mississippi. Unfortunately, a rather tall, ugly wall has been built to protect the area from flood, so the view lacks something—water, to be exact. There is an opening and a deck you can drive onto to enjoy the sights, though, if you are fond of rivers—and who isn't? There's just something about the power of that big river.

About a block away is what will probably be your favorite place if you have any Cajun instincts at all. ◆ **Broussard's Cajun Restaurant** even has a test on the back of the menu to see if there is a trace of Cajun blood in your veins. The "How to tell a full-blooded, dipped-in-the-bayou Cajun from someone who just wishes he was" test begins with the question "did your grandmother regularly eat *couche* for breakfast?" and ends with "if someone stepped on your toe would you yell *'ho yii'* instead of 'ouch'?" If any of you good ol' boys are missing home, this is the place for you, at 120 North Main (314–334–7235).

The food here is authentic, fire-breathing Cajun. The menu has a glossary of terms and a key to spicy foods for those of you who don't like surprises. It is an inexpensive, casual place, but take enough money to try the Cajun Combo for $10.99, which includes a little bit of everything: shrimp and crab meat gumbo, red beans and rice with sausage, and crawfish and shrimp étoufée. Also, if you have room, the special includes a salad and French bread. Other entrees range from the $4.99 all-you-can-eat red beans and rice with sausage to the fried crawfish tails for $12.99. Polish it off with the "bottomless" draft for $5.00. Sunday hours are 10:30 A.M. to 11:00 P.M.

The **Blue Bayou,** is Broussard's jazz club next door. It features a four-piece band playing blues and dance music every night. Broussard's motto is *"Laissez Les Bons Temps Rouler!"*—Let the Good Times Roll. Hours are Monday through Thursday 10:00 A.M. to 11:00 P.M., Friday and Saturday 10:00 A.M. to 1:30 A.M., and Sunday 4:00 P.M. to 10:00 P.M.

Near Cape Girardeau, grits begin to sneak onto the breakfast menu, and the accent begins to sound slightly more Southern than Midwestern.

On Highway 61 South, watch the signs for ◆ **Lambert's Cafe** in Sikeston, home of "throwed rolls." Lambert's, at 2515 East Malone (314–471–4261), is a most unusual place. Yes, they do throw rolls at Lambert's.

It all began on a busy day in May 1976 when passing rolls real nice-like got too slow and a customer hollered, "Just throw me the *x*#! thing!" Before you could say "thank you kindly," others cried out for service, and they have been throwing rolls at Lambert's ever since.

The folks here take control of your dinner needs—and control is the right word (got to have it when you're lobbing a long one). Want another roll? Sing out and look alive, because one will come whizzing by. To complement the rolls thrown your way, another ladleful of sorghum (Missouri's answer to Vermont maple syrup) will be slopped onto your roll, which is already dripping butter. This will require a trip to the restroom to unstick your fingers. Lambert's is fun—if you like noise and confusion—and a lot of food and attention from the waiters.

If your plate begins to look empty, someone comes by with a ladle of beans, or fried okra, or applesauce and plops it in the middle of your plate; when you finish dinner, you will be full. Very, very full. Then you will discover that they are famous for the size of their slices of homemade pie and cobbler. The drinks are served in gallon Mason jars and the atmosphere is a madhouse on a good day, but it's a spot you can talk about for years. Hours are 10:30 A.M. until 9:00 P.M. seven days a week.

OLD MOUNTAIN REGION

Now you have a choice—go south to the bootheel or loop back up toward St. Louie. West on Highway 60 toward Dexter, the flat, Kansas-like real estate will begin to curve again in the distance.

Maybe you saw geese in the air and heard their wild cries as you ate your frog's legs. A short trip will take you through Puxico to ◆**Mingo National Wildlife Refuge,** a vital 21, 676–acre link in the chain of refuges along the Mississippi flyway.

The hills flatten into wetlands and plant varieties change visibly. Mingo Swamp was formed some 18,000 years ago when the Mississippi abandoned its bed, leaving an oxbow that filled in with dense swamp species. Abundant artifacts point to the area's use by Native Americans, drawn here by swamp-loving wildlife. (No artifacts can be removed from Mingo, however, so arrowhead hunters, take note.)

The area offers boardwalk nature trails and a chance to see wildlife in its natural habitat. There is a resident waterfowl flock as well as thousands of seasonal migrants, and two active bald eagle nests are located on the refuge. Be sure to stop by the refuge visitors' center before heading into the swamp (especially during the winter months), not only to let someone know where you are going, but to enjoy the interpretive displays. Call (314) 222–3589.

Together with the adjacent Duck Creek Wildlife Area, a state wildlife management area, this is the largest hardwood swamp remaining in the state. Lake Wappapello is also nearby; watch for signs.

If you don't expect to find a museum of fine art in the Ozarks, you're in for a surprise. The ❖**Margaret Harwell Art Museum** in Poplar Bluff boasts a growing collection of works by contemporary Missouri artists.

Housed in a beautiful 1883 home, the museum has mounted one-man shows by important artists such as sculptor Ernest Trova, Swedish artist Anders Zorn, and Missourian Thomas Hart Benton. There is no charge to view the two exhibits. The museum focuses on themes ranging from contemporary photography to fiber art and recognizes the importance of the native arts of the Ozark region. It has held exhibits of folk art including quilting and basket making. It is the only art center within a 90–mile radius and the only art museum within 150 miles of Poplar Bluff. Docents conduct regular tours of the exhibit. The museum, at 427 North Main, is closed Monday and Tuesday. Call (314) 686–8002 for information. Hours are 1:00 to 4:00 P.M.

BOOTHEEL REGION

Southeast of Sikeston you'll find hills that really roll. ❖**Big Oak Tree State Park** tells the story of the 1811 New Madrid earthquake, which altered the topography of the southeast lowlands. All the land from Cape Girardeau south to Helena, Arkansas, sank from 10 to 50 feet, flooding most of what is now New Madrid, Pemiscot, and Dunklin counties. Rich Bootheel forests were converted to swampland, providing temporary protection for the giant tree. You may see trees 120 to 130 feet tall. Enjoy a bayou setting for picnics or fishing. Big Oak Tree is east off Highway 102.

Nearby ❖**Towosahgy State Historic Site** (off Highway 77) is sixty-four acres of prehistory. Archaeologists believe the site was inhabited between A.D. 1000 and A.D. 1400. Although other groups had lived in this area before that time, their societies did not reach such a highly organized level as that of the Indians at Towosahgy. Experts believe their use of the

Mississippi for trade and transportation contributed to this advancement. The river was the link between Towosahgy and the ceremonial center near the present site of Cahokia, Illinois.

Cotton fields join wheat fields as you approach New Madrid (that's pronounced *MAD-rid,* much more Midwestern than Spanish) on Interstate 55. The Mississippi River Observation Deck offers a panoramic view of the New Madrid oxbow; 8 miles of river are visible from the top of the most perfect oxbow on the Mississippi.

The oldest city west of the Mississippi (see, there's that claim again) has something for everyone. Begin at 1 Main Street. This building, on the banks of the Mississippi near the new observation deck, was once the First and Last Chance Saloon. There were no roads to New Madrid; all the traffic came off the mighty river. Here was the first—and last—chance to get a drink back in 1783. It is now the New Madrid Historical Museum.

New Madrid looks sleepy, dreaming away beside the river. It looks safe. It looks as if nothing much could happen here— indeed, as if nothing much ever had. If that's what you think when you see the place, you're wrong.

It balances precariously on one of the most active earthquake faults on the continent. In 1811, the balance shifted. The earth shrugged. The mighty Mississippi was suddenly dammed and ran backward, boats broke up and sank at their moorings, homes disintegrated before their owners' horrified eyes. John James Audubon recounted a hilarious—if frightening—tale of a wedding party broken up by the quake, and the naturalist John Bradbury described it in harrowing scientific detail as he calmly watched the earth come apart. The quake was so violent that it rang church bells in Boston.

All is not peace and quiet, even now. Howell says that there is a measurable tremor on the seismographs almost every day that can be felt by local folks. The Center for Earthquake Studies at Southeast Missouri State University informs us that a major quake is not just possible, but inevitable; stresses within the earth slowly mount until something has to give. When it does, there will be damage over an area more than twenty times that affected by a California quake because of the underlying geologic conditions—the ground will literally liquefy.

Residents have developed a wonderful gallows humor—you'd have to! T-shirts read, with a certain quirky pride, "It's Our

Hunter-Dawson Home, New Madrid

Fault" and "Visit New Madrid—while it's still here." So, you want real excitement? Head for New Madrid. (Of course, the authors file a disclaimer here. If there's a quake while you're in town, it's "not our fault.")

While in New Madrid, visit the ◆ **Hunter-Dawson Home and Historic Site.** Built in 1859 by William Washington Hunter, this crisp white house with its ornate trim and contrasting shutters recalls a more genteel era. The costumed guides who answer all your questions treat you with that special Southern charm and add to the atmosphere. A small admission fee is charged.

As you continue south from Sikeston and New Madrid, the land becomes flat bottomland. Southern-style cotton, soybeans, and peaches are the important crops here. From Kennett and Malden on the west to Hayti and Caruthersville on the east, hospitality is just what you would expect in this area of Southern heritage, and Missouri begins to feel like Dixie. Welcome, y'all.

Southwest Missouri

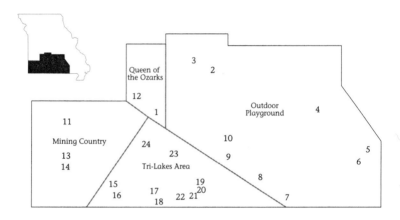

1. Bass Pro Shops Outdoor World
2. The Puzzle Source
3. Big Piney River National Scenic Trail Rides
4. Ozark National Scenic Riverways
5. Jackie's Country Store
6. Big Spring Lodge
7. Grand Gulf State Park
8. Zanoni Mill Inn Bed and Breakfast
9. Assumption Abbey
10. Laura Ingalls Wilder–Rose Wilder Lane Museum and Home
11. Maple Lane Farm
12. Red Oak II
13. George Washington Carver National Monument
14. The Real Hatfield Smokehouse
15. Devil's Kitchen Trail
16. Roaring River State Park
17. Omega Pottery Shop
18. Woodcarvings Unlimited
19. Shepherd of the Hills Inspiration Tower
20. Branson Scenic Railway
21. Stone Hill Wine Company
22. School of the Ozarks
23. Cathedral Church of the Prince of Peace
24. Ozark

SOUTHWEST MISSOURI

Mark Twain National Forest covers thousands of acres of south-west Missouri. Hundreds of miles of hiking and horseback trails free you from even the small, state-maintained highways. If you wander too far off the beaten path here, you will find yourself lost in the woods (and Missouri's bright bluebirds and crimson cardinals will clean up your trail of breadcrumbs).

Many of the lovely, quick-running streams are designated National Scenic Riverways, and the "tri-lakes" area has water, water everywhere. Resort towns are crowded in the summer and deserted in winter. Spring and fall (while school's in session) are just right for exploration. Campgrounds and canoe rentals are everywhere, and there are both gentle rivers for floating and white water for adventure.

If caves are fascinating to you, if you like spectacular rock for-mations, or if you collect rocks or minerals, southwest Missouri will keep you busy. Truitt's Cave at Lanagan, Ozark Wonder Cave at Noel, the Tiff Mines near Seneca, and the Carthage Marble Quarry at Carthage are a few spots you'll want to check.

Bed and breakfast fans can write Kay Cameron at Ozark Mountain Country Bed and Breakfast Service, Box 295, Branson 65616. You can call her, too, at (417) 334–4720 or (800) 321–8594 for a list of B&Bs in the area. She loves matchmaking and finding just exactly the right place for you.

QUEEN OF THE OZARKS

The hub of southwest Missouri is Springfield on Interstate 44, the state's third-largest city. Its location on the large grassy uplands of Grand Prairie and Kickapoo Prairie, the rural land-scape of the Springfield Plain, is one of the most beautiful in Missouri.

Here's a happy combination of forests, free-running water, and magnificent rock outcrops dotting a farmland that resem-bles the bluegrass area of Kentucky. Herefords, Black Angus, Charolais, and Simmental graze in the cleared uplands. Lesped-ezas, orchard grass, and fescue glaze the gently rolling pastures with green.

At the east edge of Springfield's Commercial Street Historic District, a small brick building houses the **Frisco Railroad Museum.** Its founder, Alan Schmitt, has a passion for the railroad system that employed his grandfather and most of the men in his wife's family. Alan grew up with the sound of the locomotives and clashing of couplers lulling him to sleep at night. By the 1970s, he had acquired enough Frisco memorabilia to build a train station in his basement. His hobby was fast becoming too big for his home, and his dream became a museum. He gathered others into his dream by forming a committee of former Frisco employees, model railroaders, and collectors. Driven by his enthusiasm in 1986, five years after Burlington Northern and Frisco merged killing the Frisco line—the Frisco was brought back to life. The first museum opened in a detached garage next to Schmitt's house, the committee became a board of directors, and an organization called Frisco Folks with a newsletter fashioned after the old Frisco employee magazine *All Aboard* was launched. Soon photos and memorabilia began to flow in from all over the country. In six months more than one thousand items had arrived, and the museum had outgrown the garage. Soon the railroad closed its last shop in Springfield and donated all the files filled with information and specifications on everything from locomotive design to depot architecture. Schmitt and the board began the search for the perfect building.

With the help of a successful fund-raiser, the Frisco's old centralized traffic control command center reopened as the Frisco Museum. But there is even more to this happy ending for railroad buffs. A new 9,000–square-foot building adjacent to the current museum is being built. It will be filled with fifty life-size dioramas fashioned after the Smithsonian's Museum of American History. It will include a mock-up of an old brick engine house. On its mezzanine level, a 2,000–square-foot model railroad layout will operate. An observation deck will overlook Burlington Northern's tracks just below. Oh, and the little newsletter is now a slick twenty-page magazine. It reminds you of *The Little Engine That Could.* Museum hours are from 10:00 A.M. until 5:00 P.M., Tuesday through Saturday. Call (417) 866-7573 for more information.

Okay, ❖ **Bass Pro Shops Outdoor World** at 1935 South Campbell—a major intersection in Springfield—is rather on the track. It bills itself as the world's greatest sporting goods store, then lives up to that boast. How many sports shops have a two-story log cabin right in the store? Or a sumptuous restaurant like Hemingway's, serving lobster dinner and a glass of fine wine in front of a room-size aquarium (with white-bellied sharks smiling through the glass and a 15–foot eel hiding in the filter system)?

Across the aerial walkway from Hemingway's is the old-fashioned Tall Tales Barbershop. There is original wildlife art, a museum of the outdoors, trophy animals by the hundreds, and the biggest live bass in captivity. You can buy a hand-knit sweater, get wet beside an indoor waterfall, practice with your new shotgun in the shooting range downstairs, and buy a pair of gym shoes or a fishing rod. Just plan on spending a couple of hours when you go in, and take a camera—there are photo opportunities indicated everywhere; you can pose with 10–foot black bears or tiny fawns. There was a fire at Bass Pro Shops that destroyed part of the south end, but rest assured, the rest is all still there.

Springfield is a major city, but, as in most big cities, there are hidden treasures. Karol and Nancy Brown's **Walnut Street Inn Bed and Breakfast** at 900 East Walnut (417–864–6346) has a quiet ambience to counter the big-city feel. Each of the eleven rooms includes a private bath, some with original porcelain antique fixtures, hardwood floors, and antique furnishings. Ozark specialties such as persimmon muffins and walnut bread are featured along with a full breakfast. Rates are $80 to $135 per night for two persons.

Aesthetic Concerns, Ltd., at 326 Boonville (417–864–4177) is the kind of place that is difficult to find outside a city. It is filled with the things needed to restore an old home or to give character to a new one—fixtures, plumbing, chandeliers, and architectural details. Tom M. Hembree and Tim Gregory, owners of this collection of unique antiques, keep hours from 10:00 A.M. to 6:00 P.M. Monday through Saturday.

An outstanding nature center, designed by the Missouri Department of Conservation, is at 4600 South Chrisman (417–882–4237). Want to know how to tell a hawk from a heron when they're far overhead? David Catlin, manager of the center, or one of the volunteers will show you silhouettes suspended from the ceiling that correspond to identifying shapes on the floor. Another room invites you into the dark with displays that light up—or sing out—as you press a button or break a light beam. See a barred owl, hear a whippoorwill, watch a flying squirrel—it's all here. Outdoor nature trails take you through Ozark woodlands and a small bog; learn while you take in the fresh air.

Springfield is a mecca for watercolorists. For thirty-five years, the **Springfield Art Museum** (417–866–2716) has been the locus for Watercolor USA, one of the most prestigious shows in the nation. Every June and July the museum displays the best and the brightest; you may browse or buy at 1111 Brookside. (You'll know you're close when you see the large yellow sculpture called "Sun Target"; local kids call it "The French Fries.") The museum owns a fine permanent collection of original works. Visit at any time of the year. Museum hours are Sunday from 1:00 to 5:00 P.M.; Tuesday, Wednesday, and Saturday from 9:00 A.M. to 5:00 P.M.; and Thursday and Friday from 9:00 A.M. until 8:00 P.M.

Outdoor Playground

Just outside Springfield on Highway 65 is another kind of mecca—tiny Galloway is wall-to-wall antiques. It's as if the town had been invaded by aliens selling oldies; nearly every building and home is now a shop. Find everything from a vine-and-thorn-wrapped birdhouse (to discourage cats, of course) to European china, but don't stop before you get to the flea market a half-mile or so north of the other shops. Here are two floors of great bargain flea market antiques.

Ten miles or so north of Springfield on Highway 65 is the little town of Fair Grove, with its restored buildings full of craftspeople and shops. It's only three or four blocks off 65; slow down or you'll miss it. Watch for **Mercantile Antiques,** an old storefront building that features antiques as well as pottery and the fine overshot weaving of Marge Wallis, among other things. Through the week, you'll catch the crafters from 10:00 A.M. until 5:00 P.M. Not to worry though, if you're passing through on a Sunday afternoon, you'll find them open for business from noon until 5:00 P.M. (417) 759–7794.

Head north on Interstate 44 to Lebanon, a town loaded with surprises. Flea markets and antiques shops are all over the place, more than twenty-three at last count.

✦**The Puzzle Source** is not for everyone, but if you are a jigsaw puzzle fan, this is a must. Keith and Nancy Ballhagen have the only jigsaw puzzle shop in the Ozarks, with the world's smallest puzzle (2¼ inches by 2½ inches with 99 pieces) and the world's largest puzzle (3½ feet by 9 feet, 7,500 pieces). There are double-sided puzzles, round puzzles, and puzzles within puzzles. Movie poster puzzles, postage stamp puzzles, and puzzles covering any subject you can think of. The most popular is the Route 66 puzzle (600 pieces). Nancy says they just always liked to do puzzles, especially when the children were young, and it sort of grew into a business. They have more than 1,200 puzzles displayed in their shop and now are carving wooden puzzles. To find puzzle paradise, take exit 135 (Sleeper exit) from Interstate 44 and follow the east outer road ¾ mile to the first mailbox on your left—you can see it from the freeway. Hours are 8:00 A.M. to 6:00 P.M. during the summer and 9:00 A.M. to 5:00 P.M. in the winter, or call (417) 286–3837.

Log Cabin Canoe and Outfitters, Chuck and Wanda Robbins's campground (417–532–6439), near Lebanon and Moon Valley, is snuggled between the Niangua River and beautiful high bluffs off Highway 64 east of Lebanon. This campground tries to separate church groups and scouts from "party people" to make happy campers of everyone. Not just a campground and rental place, they offer a package float trip that comes with a cookout breakfast, free showers and firewood, a dinner barbecue, and a hayride for the kids. If you have never been canoeing, southwest Missouri is the place to try it. There is water suitable for beginners as well as white water for the more experienced, year-round floating, and April through October camping.

A small side trip north on Interstate 44 will quickly take you to Waynesville and the ✦**Big Piney River National Scenic Trail Rides** there. This is a chance to get off the roads and into the woods. Ride well-mannered horses over mountains, through beautiful valleys, along the edge of bluffs, through quiet forests, and along the famous Big Piney River. Rental horses are available for $30 a day plus the regular fee ($30 a day or $150 for six days). Evening entertainment includes horse shows, movies, square dancing, family games, and good wholesome outdoor recreational activities. From May through October the Jerry Laughlin family plans six-day rides. Campsites have a dining hall, modern rest rooms, showers, and electricity. Sunday church services are held in a dining hall and on the trail. Arrangements must be made in advance, so call (314) 774–6879, or (314) 774–2986.

Fort Leonard Wood is the home of the U.S. Army Corps of Engineers. It is also the home of the Army Engineering Center and the **U.S. Army Engineer Museum.** The Fort covers about 63,000 acres in the Ozarks about 130 miles southwest of St. Louis on I-44 near Waynesville. A recipe for creamed chipped beef on toast, called S.O.S by the soldiers who had to eat it, is tacked on the wall of a restored mess hall, one of several "temporary" wooden buildings built during World War II. A field kitchen lists the Fort's daily food requirements in 1943. These included 4,750 pounds of bacon, 47 gallons of vinegar and 105 gallons of syrup.

The oldest treasure is a signet ring that belonged to Lysimachus, an engineer general who served Alexander the Great in about 330 B.C. The museum walks people through a chronological history of the Corps. There are several specialized galleries. Many of the temporary mobilization buildings, two-story wooden barracks familiar to soldiers at every post in the world and built to last about 10 years, have been restored to create typical company areas. A supply room with a wood-burning stove, racks for M1 rifles and 45–caliber pistols, and entrenching tools would bring a tear to a supply sergeant's eye.

The history of the Corps, however, dates back to the Revolutionary War. There's a 1741 muzzle-loading cannon that the French lent to the Continental Army, and a shovel and ax dating from the 1781 battle of Yorktown, the first engineering victory of army engineers who built fortifications and trenches into British positions. The oldest unit in the U.S. Army is the 101st Engineer Battalion of the Massachusetts National Guard established in 1636.

Another display demonstrates low tide at Omaha Beach during the D-Day invasion of June 6, 1944, with an engineer disposing of German mines that would have been a danger to Allied ships.

Children can take the wheel of a restored pilothouse, U.S. Snag Boat No. 13, which kept the Mississippi River clear for more than 50 years. Other hands-on activities include a land-mine detector. Gun enthusiasts will enjoy the nineteenth-century Gatling Gun, an 1819 Flintlock rifle, an 1816 Springfield 69–caliber musket, and many small arms from more recent wars.

The museum is at the corner of Nebraska and South Dakota avenues. Hours are 10:00 A.M. to 4:00 P.M. Monday through Saturday. Admission is free but donations are accepted. Call (314) 596–0169 for more information.

Wander down Highway VV from Licking and enjoy the rugged countryside, which contains some of the largest springs in the world. The Jacks Fork River, Alley Spring with its restored "Old Red Mill," and the Current River near Eminence provide year-round canoeing. (The spring water is a consistent fifty-eight degrees year-round.)

Alley Spring Mill was closed a few summers back for restoration and is now open every day from Memorial Day through Labor day from 9:00 A.M. until 4:00 P.M. Rangers are on hand to explain how the mill worked, and the role it played in developing a community of Ozark settlers. The area still calls people together as it has for more than 10,000 years. Native Americans gathered here to hunt the abundant game and fish the rich waters. The first mill was built in 1868. A newer one replaced it in 1894. The latter was cutting edge in its technology, featuring a turbine rather than a water wheel, and rollers to replace the grist stones. Soon a blacksmith opened a shop and people began to gather here and camp with entire families while the grain was ground. Now it is a popular spot for family reunions, camp outs, and fishing trips. Camping and canoe rentals are available at the mill, which is located 6 miles west of Eminence on State Route 106. For more details call (314) 323–4236.

Missouri's southwestern rivers—quick-running, spring-fed and bone-chillingly cold—are so beautiful they bring a lump to your throat. In fact, the Current, the Eleven Point, and the Jacks Fork have been designated ❖**Ozark National Scenic Riverways.**

Generations of canoeists and trout fishermen know these secluded waters. You can spend the day without seeing another soul, then camp on a quiet sandbar at day's end and listen to the chuck-will's-widows and owls call while your fire lights the riffles with bronze. Pick fresh watercress from these icy waters to garnish the trout that sizzles in lemon butter on your grill, and know that life gets no better than this. There are plenty of rental outfits; pick up brochures anywhere.

Springs gush from beneath solid rock, slowly carving themselves a cave. Early residents built mills here to produce flour, cornmeal, and sawn lumber. There's as much natural history as history along these bright rivers.

Alley Spring Mill is called the most picturesque spot in the state. Some eighty million gallons of water a day flow through here, and the Red Mill has been restored to working order.

Big Spring is the largest concentration of springs in the world, which is a mystery to hydrologists who do not understand the large volume of water. Beautiful rivers gush right out of the ground from the base of spectacular rock bluffs and create the most consistent, spring-fed, crystal-clear rivers in the country. Round Spring Cave is just off Highway 19.

If you have horses, **Cross Country Trail Rides** has a week planned for you. You can take the whole family on a cross-country trail ride in April, May, June, August, October, or December. Jim and Jane Smith have spent thirty-five years perfecting the week's adventure. You will camp for the week on Jacks Fork River. The ride leaves and returns to the base camp every night, where eighteen meals are served and entertainment is royal. Well-known country music performers entertain at a dance every night but Sunday. There are horse shows, team roping events, and other sports to show off your steed. Jane says they fill up months in advance; to ensure a spot, write P.O. Box 15, Eminence 65466, or call (314) 226–3492. The cost is $160 for each adult (lower rates for kids), and there is a $5.00 tie-stall or $10.00 barn-stall reservation for your proud mount. This is a "B.Y.O.H." affair; no rental horses are available.

A winding drive along Highway 160 takes you to the beautiful Eleven Point River, with its many natural springs and lovely spots for picnics. You will be surprised at the excellent roads through these wooded hills. The Between the Rivers section of the Ozark Hiking Trail covers about 30 miles. The northern entry point to this section is on Highway 60 approximately 3½ miles west of Van Buren. Trailhead parking is provided for users at Highway 60 and at Sinking Creek Lookout Tower about a mile west of Highway J.

The trail winds south for the first 13 miles across small tributaries that feed the Current River. Creeks with names such as Wildhorse Hollow, Devil's Run, and Big Barren flow through the area. Designed for both hikers and horses, the trail crosses a ridge that divides the Current River from the Eleven Point River along

Gold Mine Hollow. The trail offers panoramic mountain views and deeply wooded areas to filter the summer sun. If you are a hiking enthusiast, this area is for you. Pick up a book with a listing of all the hiking trails on federal property, complete with maps, at the Federal Forest Service Office in Winona, grab your backpack, and head out.

Wooded Ozark roads stretch out before you now, with oak trees shouldering evergreens; the Doniphan Lookout Tower watches the national forest for fires here. Tune your AM radio to 1610 for Ozark Riverway information if you are headed for canoeing or camping at one of the many parks or rivers nearby.

Because of the number of campers who take this route to the wilderness, the little town of Van Buren on Highway 60 is the home of several neat shops. ✦**Jackie's Country Store** at the corner of Main and John streets is owned by Jackie Wilson, who has lived in Van Buren for almost twenty-three years. "It's a whole different lifestyle," she says of the tiny town. She is from the Kansas City area; now she lives in a house overlooking a river and says she wouldn't live anywhere else. Pick up smoked meats, cheeses, and natural foods as well as deli sandwiches, fresh flowers, and gifts at this country store.

Jackie has a large pickle jar on the counter and time to chat; the sign on the door says OPEN WHEN I GET HERE, CLOSED WHEN I GET TIRED, and that says something about the lifestyle here. The hours translate to around 9:00 A.M. to 5:00 P.M. (314–323–8560).

✦**Big Spring Lodge** (314–323–4423) is about 4 miles from Van Buren; it is a National Park Service site on the Ozark National Scenic Riverways. Rustic log cabins with fireplaces that reflect a more relaxed pace and a dining lodge/craft shop were built by the Civilian Conservation Corps (the CCC, otherwise known as "Roosevelt's Tree Army") in the thirties. The lodge is on the National Register, and rightly so; log, timber, rocks, and cut stone materials and unique spatial arrangements make this an excellent example of the projects that brought work to so many in Depression-era America. Dining room hours vary with the season. For more information write Big Spring Lodge, P.O. Box 602, Van Buren 63965.

Big Spring State Park is nearby, as are the Mark Twain National Forest and the Ozark National Riverways Tourist Information Station. Call (314) 323–4236 or write in advance for an accurate list of trails and starting points (P.O. Box 490, Van Buren 63965). Also, any Missouri tourism office can provide a list of hiking trails.

Big Spring is the largest single spring in the world, pouring out 277 million gallons of crystal-clear water each day—a breathtaking natural wonder you will want to photograph or draw.

The beginnings of ✦ **Grand Gulf State Park** (Missouri's answer to the Grand Canyon) in Thayer go back 450 million years to a time when sediment was deposited by ancient seas, forming dolomitic rock. As the area uplifted and the sea receded, water percolated down through cracks in the rock and began to dissolve passageways underneath. Streams cut their own beds on the surface of the soft rock. As air-filled caves formed and cave roofs collapsed, streams were diverted underground. The collapse of the Grand Gulf occurred within the past 10,000 years—fairly recent by a geologist's reckoning.

Today the gulf is ¾ mile wide with side walls 120 feet high. Part of the cave roof that did not collapse formed a natural bridge 75 feet high that spans 200 feet, one of the largest in the state. The park contains handicapped accessible overlooks with spectacular views of the chasm, a ¼–mile loop trail around the gulf, and a primitive trail across the rock bridge (don't look down!). Call (314) 548–2525 for details.

West Plains is a starting point for canoeing on the North Fork River. Or you can strike off on foot into the wilderness of the Mark Twain National Forest.

Travel westbound from West Plains on Highway 160 to Highway 181 north to the little town of Zanoni if you want total peace, quiet, and privacy with nothing to disturb your sleep but the morning song of bluebirds and wrens.

The ✦ **Zanoni Mill Inn Bed and Breakfast** is a modern home set beside the remnants of an Ozark pioneer village in a secluded valley with a private lake. It has four large bedrooms, two with connecting baths and two with hall baths. All rooms have queen-size beds, but that is only the beginning of the amenities offered here. How about an 18–foot x 36–foot indoor pool and a hot tub, where you can soak and watch the big-screen TV? There is Ping-Pong and pool in the game room. But most interesting is the old mill itself, powered since the Civil War by the spring still gushing out of the hillside, restored and now owned by the great-grandchildren of the original 1870 settlers, and maintained by the grandson of the man who built the present mill in 1905 (the first two burned) to grind corn and wheat. Dave and Mary Morrison turn out a big country breakfast every day, because the home is headquarters of a 1,750–acre working ranch, and that requires a large breakfast, served by the pool if you like. Call (417) 679–4050, or Ozark Mountain Country Reservation Service at (800) 695–1546. Rooms are $65 per night.

Go west on highway 160 on some roller-coaster-style roads to reach this out-of-the-way resort **Turkey Creek Ranch.** Near Theodosia, it sits on a hill overlooking Bull Shoals Lake on the edge of a 400–acre working ranch. The resort has twenty-four cottages all with screened porches and squeaky clean kitchens. There are indoor and outdoor pools and lighted boat dock. You can take horses into the surrounding hills. Owners Dick and Elda Edwards bought a rundown farm more than forty years ago and now have a popular resort that even has a small restaurant. Cost of cottages range from $77 to $125 a day. Call (417) 273–4362 for more information.

Deep in the Ozark hills near Ava a bell chimes in the early morning quiet. Trappist monks in white robes and cowls move quietly into the darkness of the chapel for morning prayer and meditation. A day begins at ❖ **Assumption Abbey,** one of only eighteen monasteries of the Trappist order in the country. The abbey is surrounded by 3,400 wooded acres. The monks seldom leave the abbey and by their simple lives of prayer, labor, study, and solitude seek a deeper personal relationship with God. So why mention a monastery in a travel guide, you might ask? Well, although man cannot live by bread alone, a visit to the Assumption Abbey bakery is in order. To be self-supporting as monasteries must, the monks discovered a market for fruitcakes. Now they produce more than 18,000 fruitcakes annually. The old English recipe is mixed in the tiny kitchen of the abbey. Each cake weighs two pounds and is generously filled with raisins, cherries, and pineapple marinated in Burgundy. Each one is bathed with an ounce of dark rum for moistness and flavor. They bear no resemblance to the ready-made kind you get from your aunt at Christmas. They are sold by direct mail to customers all over the United States and are carried at prestigious stores such as Williams-Sonoma and Neiman-Marcus.

The abbey extends hospitality to men and women of all

Laura Ingalls Wilder Home and Museum, Mansfield

faiths. If you need a restful weekend, or counseling from the monks, you are welcome. Guests get home-cooked meals served family-style by the brothers. There is no charge for meals or accommodations due to the monks' vows to remain poor and serve others. Advance reservations for overnight stays are requested and donations help with the expenses. The simple quarters contain wash basins, twin beds, shared bath/shower, and a small homemade desk. Monks bring fresh soap and towels. It is a simple life. If you would like to spend a few days at this retreat, call (417) 683–2258 or write Rt. 5 Box 1056, Ava, MO 65608.

North on Highway 5 is tiny Mansfield, home of the ✦ **Laura Ingalls Wilder-Rose Wilder Lane Museum and Home** (417–924–3626). Laura's home is just as she left it and there is a museum that contains four handwritten manuscripts. Author of the now famous (courtesy of television) *Little House on the Prairie,* among other books, Laura was encouraged to write by her daughter, Rose Wilder Lane, a well-known author in her own right from the early 1900s. They are buried in the Mansfield cemetery.

There are several B&Bs in and around Mansfield. The **Dickey House** in Mansfield is a stately three-story Colonial Revival mansion. The four guest rooms are filled with antiques. Each has a private bath; two have queen-sized beds and two have double beds. The rooms share a screened balcony. This is a comfortable adult getaway, and a full breakfast is included. Call Ozark Mountain Country Reservation Service, (800) 695–1546 for current prices.

Dairyland Bed & Breakfast is 18 miles west of Mansfield near Seymour. It is a private home on a working dairy farm with your family as their exclusive guests. Guests have use of the living room, two bedrooms with queen and double beds, and an equipped kitchen. A fine Continental breakfast is served every morning. The price is $60 for two persons; $15 for each additional person. Of course, children are welcome, that's the whole point of staying on a working ranch (under age twelve add $10 for each each). Call Ozark Mountain Country Reservation Service (800) 695–1546 for more information.

Go west on Highway 60 to swing back into Springfield.

MINING COUNTRY

Head west on Interstate 44 to Halltown; then slip onto Highway 96 west for Carthage, where the majestic 1895 Jasper County Court House stands proudly on the square, turreted like a medieval castle. Settled in the 1840s, Carthage was burned to the ground in guerrilla raids during the Civil War. Lead and zinc mines were developed after the war and wealthy owners built magnificent homes away from the mining camps. Marble quarries provided Carthage gray marble for many large state and federal buildings. The fine old homes found here bespeak prosperity. It's still a beautiful city—the courthouse, high school, and many of the churches and homes are built of the stone quarried here. (The stone is not technically marble, but a limestone that takes a high polish.) Both the courthouse and high school contain murals by Lowell Davis, one of America's most well-known nature artists and a native of Carthage.

Carthage has more than its share of well-known native sons and is becoming a center for artists in the area. About eighteen resident artists call it home. Internationally known zoologist and naturalist Marlin Perkins (remember "Wild Kingdom"?) was born here; you'll find a bronze sculpture of Perkins by artists Bob Tommey and Bill Snow in Central Park on Garrison Avenue.

Follow the historic drive markers for a tour of the magnificent old mansions that have been kept so beautifully over the years. Innkeepers Nolan and Nancy Henry welcome you to their home, the imposing **Leggett House,** at 1106 Grand (417–358–0683). Nancy and Nolan are from Kansas City. They saw the house, which was in sad repair, and bought it. Nancy says that with their children grown, they needed a hobby—so they moved to Carthage and began restoring the three-story stone mansion. Now it is in its glory again with stained glass, a mosaic-tiled solarium with a marble fountain, finely crafted woodwork and—an elevator. Rates are $55 a night, which includes a full breakfast in the formal dining room.

◆**Maple Lane Farm** (417–358–6312), slightly outside of town, is a twenty-two-room Victorian bed and breakfast, complete with animals ranging from horses to pygmy goats to a Sicilian donkey. Arch and Renee (pronounced *REE-nee)* Brewer have seven grown children and many, many grandchildren. Because of the crowd coming home for holidays, the Brewers close at Christmas and Thanksgiving. But the rest of the year their three-story home is open. Deer, turkey, and quail hunting are available. The Brewers offer tours daily at 2:00 P.M. or by appointment. The place is furnished with family heirlooms. Rates are $45 a night with breakfast.

◆ **Red Oak II** is about 5 miles north of Carthage off Highway 96. This is the home of Lowell Davis, the Missouri artist/ farmer who changes "do-nothing" farm animals into spirited creatures with a world of personality that have caught the imagination of the country. His forty-acre Foxfire Farm was "the ugliest farm in the county" when he and wife Charlie bought it, Davis said in a *Saturday Evening Post* article. It has been transformed into what he calls a "time-warp illusion"; a perfect replica of a 1930s farm—buildings, machinery, tools, and all. When Davis goes to shows around the country, he takes a wonderful old huckster's wagon filled with art supplies and memorabilia.

Now Davis has built the town of Red Oak II off historic Route 66—Missouri Highway 96. Whenever Davis found an old building falling down, he would pick it up and move it to Red Oak, creating a town in a cornfield that feels like his old home town. Now the town has everything you need—church, school, general store, sawmill, feed store, gas station, and blacksmith shop. There are barns, chicken coops (with chickens), corn cribs, old wooden homes surrounded by white picket fences (and privies, of course). It has become a low-key tourist attraction, drawing several dozen people a day. Davis's sculptures and paintings are for sale at the general store, and he has converted four old homes into bed and breakfast inns.

The abandoned tailing piles and mine shafts scattered about the town and the elegant homes just west of the downtown area are reminders of the mining era of Joplin. Mineral collectors are drawn to the abandoned mine dumps and chert piles and to the mineral museum in Schifferdecker Park, one of the best museums of its kind in the state.

Outside Joplin go east on County Highway V to Diamond. From Diamond, drive 2 miles on V and then south about a mile to find the ◆ **George Washington Carver National Monument,** which commemorates a man who was more than an educator, botanist, agronomist, and "cookstove chemist." He was the man who wanted "to be of the greatest good to the greatest number of people," a man who refused to accept boundaries, who drew from science, art, and religion to become a teacher and director of a department at Tuskegee Institute in Alabama. He taught botany and agriculture to the children of ex-slaves and tried to devise farming methods to improve the land exhausted by cotton. Known as the "Peanut Man," Carver led poor, one-horse farmers to grow protein-rich and soil-regenerating soybeans and peanuts. The Carver Nature Trail leads from the birthplace site through two springs and ends at the Carver family cemetery.

Just down Highway 71 is ◆ **The Real Hatfield Smokehouse** (417–624–3765). Owner Nick Neece has a sparkle in his blue eyes as he talks about his "home-grown" hogs. "We smoke anything you can get from a hog," he says. Bacon, hams—you name it, he smokes it. He will mail hams anywhere in the United States, and even has a regular customer in London. The small smokehouse uses a special sugar cure and hickory logs to give meats a golden brown finish and good flavor without as much salt as other smokehouses. Hours are 7:30 A.M. to 6:00

P.M. Monday through Saturday. The smokehouse is closed on Sunday.

Webb City's claim to fame, "the Praying Hands" is in King Jack Park. This 32–foot concrete-and-steel structure is atop a 40–foot-high hill. The park is named for the ore called "jack" that made the city rich in the 1870s. There are no signs inviting the visitor to stop to see the huge sculpture, it just suddenly appears. The hands were created by Jack Dawson, an art instructor at the Webb City schools, and he intended it to be just a quiet reminder for people to turn to God. Webb City is off Highway 71.

When you get enough of sitting around indoors, you outdoor folks can go west on Highway 59 at Anderson to enter canoe heaven. Highway 59 runs along the Elk River, and the sudden appearance of the famous overhanging bluffs makes you want to duck as you drive under them.

TRI-LAKES AREA

Cassville is the last town on Highway 76 before you enter the Mark Twain National Forest. It is a long and winding road through the forest, so if you arrive at this point after dark you might as well spend the night. Check out **The Rib** on Highway 112 South (417–847–3600). It's a mighty fine restaurant with a large brick fireplace to ward off the chill. Ron (known as Mack) and Mary Belle McGrath offer a super crisp salad and fine barbecue among other things on the menu.

For breakfast, there is **Dave's Cafe** on Highway 248 East (417–847–3535), where Dave and Pat Kreeger serve homemade bread, pies, and cinnamon rolls. Grits show up on the menu again in this Southern latitude, but they serve them with milk and sugar, not butter, on this side of the state. Pat starts baking at 5:30 A.M. and opens at 7:00 A.M. She and Dave serve up fried chicken for $5.00, liver and onions for $3.70 and a menu full of other goodies, all reasonably priced. Winter hours end at 7:00 P.M., but they stay open until 9:00 P.M. during the season. They are open from 7:00 A.M. until 3:00 P.M. on Sunday and are closed on Saturday.

The **◈ Devil's Kitchen Trail** winds from the valley to the top and down again, giving a close-up look at the geology and history of the area. Eleven of the park's fourteen caves are found along the rocky bench here. Shelters like these were used by Ozark bluff-dwelling Indians who lived here about 10,000 years ago. Artifacts such as food and fragments of clothing have been found to date this culture. The Devil's Kitchen was named for the stone formation that provided a hideout for Civil War Guerrillas. Headed south on Highway 112, softly winding roads, tree-lined hills, and spectacular views pop up as you crest hilltops in this lovely national forest.

❖ **Roaring River State Park** is the fountainhead of the Roaring River. There is a hidden spring in a cave filled with crystal-clear aqua blue water that stays a constant fifty-eight degrees year-round. More than 20 million gallons a day are pumped into the river. Here the state maintains a trout hatchery and stocks the river daily in season.

Roaring River State Park is part of the White River basin. From a geologist's point of view, the basin tells a fascinating story. The White River has cut into the flat Springfield plateau, creating deep, steep-walled valleys and exposing varied layers of rock— shale, limestone, dolomite, and chert.

Pastures fringed with woods are found along Highway 76 East through the Piney Creek Wildlife Area. Mile after mile of ridge roads and startling views unfold until finally, over the crest of the last hill, beautiful Table Rock Lake appears before you. It feels like the top of a ferris wheel from this vantage. The occasional small farm or Ozark stone cottage dots the roadside. Valleys with pastures, ponds, or a lone barn sitting starkly against the sky are the only traces of civilization.

At the town of Cape Fair you can turn right on Highway 76 to Table Rock Lake or turn left to Reeds Spring. Because of the proximity of Silver Dollar City, there are quite a few artists in residence. Mark Oehler's ❖ **Omega Pottery Shop** (417–272–3369) on Highway 248 East (at the south edge of town) is one of them. Mark crafts each piece of wheel-thrown stoneware and finishes it in a gas-fired kiln at 2,350 degrees—that makes it safe for oven, dishwasher, microwave, and moon missions. He travels occasionally but says it's "too much of a bother to pack everything up and move it." He would rather stay here in Reeds Spring. "Pottery is a craft that needs space to display it," he says. "That's why potters have studio-galleries."

Mark enjoys doing custom work—such as lamps, sinks, and dishes. He points to other craftspeople—Tom Hess, another potter; Lory Brown, a pine-needle basket maker; Ed Seals, who does copper work; and Kay Cloud and her wonderful Sawdust Doll Houses—all in the Reeds Spring area. Omega Pottery is open from 10:00 A.M. to 5:00 P.M. every day except Wednesday.

At the intersection of highways 248 and 13 is **Wilderness Road Clockworks and Gallery** (417–272–3256). Floor clocks in a variety of sizes, woods, and styles, including mantel, cuckoo, alarm and slab clocks, are only a very small part of what this multiroom gift shop offers. Jim Webb is the clock-repair specialist and Pat and Dean Schlobohm run the gift shop, which has dolls, trolls, and wonderful full-size carousel horses. The shop is open from 9:00 A.M. to 5:00 P.M. Monday through Saturday, noon to 5:00 P.M. on Sunday.

In the town of Kimberling City west on Highway 13 is ◆ **Woodcarvings Unlimited.** Sherry Barnes and her sister Kathy Adamson are both woodcarvers and both show their work in the shop. Kathy's Canoe Carving Shop is in her home in Bois D'Arc. Her specialty is hand-carved deck plates and yokes that are used as braces on canoes, as well as intricately carved canoe paddles. She carves river gods with long flowing beards (that resemble her husband Sonny) for the yokes of canoes. Kathy, however, doesn't just carve canoes: She works "relief carving," on pieces of flat wood and creates three-dimensional scenes. Her river series showing life along the river, look real enough to walk into. She carves mantles, clocks, and doors. She began by carving pieces for her own canoe, and the result was so beautiful that others asked her to personalize their craft.

Kathy uses teak, butternut, mahogany, cedar, and walnut, relying solely on her own strength and sharp tools to create the delicate layers in the wood. She uses earth-tone artist oils and stains to add a bit of color to the carvings while allowing the grain to show though.

Her work can also be purchased at River Madness, a canoe outfitter in Springfield, or you can commission your own personal piece by contacting Kathy. Call her at the shop, (417–739–5613), for information.

Table Rock State Park is one of the most popular (meaning crowded) state parks in Missouri. Off the beaten path here means

63

wilderness, on the path means bumper-to-bumper in summer-time. As in most resort areas in the state, early spring and late fall are perfect times to roam without the huge crowds summer brings.

Author Harold Bell Wright came to these hills for his health in the early part of this century and was so taken by the beauty of the area that he settled in to write. *The Shepherd of the Hills* is his best-known and most-beloved book; it captured the imagi-nation of generations and even became one of John Wayne's early movies (which, incidentally, borrowed only the name from the book—the script was unrecognizable!).

Highway 65 is an old-fashioned, uncrowded Ozark highway. You can still see the view as you crest hills here, but the ✦**Shepherd of the Hills Inspiration Tower** offers an incredible one. The tower's first observation level is at 145 feet; the tower is 230 feet, 10 inches tall, with two elevators or 279 stairs to the top. But rest assured it is stable. It is designed to withstand 172 mph winds (gusts of 224 mph) and it cost $1.5 million to build; this is not surprising since it contains 92,064 pounds of steel and is set in forty-three truckloads of concrete. It also contains 4,400 square feet of glass, for a breathtaking view from the highest point around the Tri-Lakes area.

If you've heard of Silver Dollar City (and you will if you stay in Missouri for long), you've heard of Branson. Once a quiet lit-tle town pocketed in the weathered Ozark Mountains near the Arkansas border, business here has picked up considerably.

Branson has changed in the past few years from the strip of country music "opries" and related foofaraw crowded cheek-by-jowl along Highway 76 to the country music capital of the Midwest, giving Nashville a run for its money. Twenty-seven theaters in town now feature such stars as Wayne Newton, Johnny Cash, Loretta Lynn, Andy Williams, Mel Tillis, and Roy Clark, who join regulars such as Boxcar Willie, Moe Bandy (the show President Bush and his staff stopped to see after the '92 GOP convention), and possibly the most popular show in town, Japanese hillbilly fiddler Shoji Tabuchi.

Branson is trying to keep up with the demand of more than four million tourists a year, but as you would suspect, about an hour before the matinee or evening shows begin, the traffic is much like a long narrow parking lot. How bad is the traffic? Well, women have been seen leaving their husbands behind the wheel on Highway 76 while they get out and shop, buy things, and rejoin their spouses in the car a block or so up the street. We are talking gridlock here. The secret to getting around is learning the back roads. Just knowing that the quickest route from Andy Williams' Theater to Ray Stevens is Forsythe Street to Truman to Shepherd of the Hills Expressway—and not 76 Country Boulevard (a road to avoid if at all possible)—can save you enough time for dinner.

There are other little secrets, too. The Chamber of Commerce will give you a free, easy-to-read map showing the shortcuts from one end of the 5-mile strip to the other. The recently repaved back roads can make life a little easier, even though you can't avoid the traffic altogether. The city now has a trolley system on the strip and that helps a bit. (Disney scouts have been looking at land around Branson for a theme park, too. That should make things even more interesting.)

Because Branson is in the throes of a building boom and the traffic can be a genuine pain, the best thing to do is to find a bed and breakfast somewhere away from Branson and then just go in when you are psyched up to do it. The paths in Branson are beaten to a fair-thee-well. Avoiding the whole place might be more to your liking. But you've come this far, so the first order of business is to get that map (Chamber of Commerce or many hotels will have them) and use all the traffic shortcuts you can. The side roads that loop off Highway 76 do reduce travel time and frustration. If you are not attending a show, stay off the streets around the 7:00 P.M. and 8:00 P.M. curtain times when about 1500 people per theater are all on Highway 76, and the local police are issuing tickets for driving in the center turn lane.

Or take the devil by the horns: stay on the strip and walk to everything. You can stroll along the strip and take the trolley. Then you can leave the driving to someone else and have fun with your friends. You and the kids can Ride The Ducks, vintage WWII amphibious vehicles that go along the strip, through an outdoor military history museum and then splash into the lake.

The Branson/Lakes Area Chamber of Commerce will send you information packets. The one to ask for is the *Branson Roads Scholar: Mastering the Back Roads of Branson*. It contains a map of alternative routes and traffic tips.

The most exciting part of visiting Branson is how easy it is to get up close to the stars, the music legends who are playing golf (10:00 A.M. on Wednesday at Pointe Royale Golf Course on Highway 165 often has Mel Tillis, Andy Williams, Moe Bandy, and Boxcar Willie teeing off together) or shopping at the grocery store. That constellation of stars is only the beginning. Other stars are scheduled to shoot through Branson for performances, too.

So you never know whom you will see sitting in one of the many restaurants (most of which are down-home sorts of places, not exactly low-calorie eateries) in town. For the best ambience, though, drive across the lake to the **Candlestick Inn** on Mt. Branson on East Seventy-sixth Street, where the food is more upscale. The atmosphere is romantic, the view of downtown Branson is sensational (especially during the Christmas season's Festival of Lights), and you never know who will be at one of the tables. The menu features such delicacies as crab-stuffed trout. You can see the humongous neon candle (says "steak and seafood") sign from downtown, but it's tricky to find if you don't know to just follow Highway 76/68 across the bridge. Call (417) 334-3633 for reservations.

Now, beyond the music shows and Silver Dollar City, there are a few other places worth seeing. **Mutton Hollow Craft Village** is a smaller and less expensive version of Silver Dollar City near 76 Country Boulevard and Shepherd of the Hills Expressway. There are thirty-eight shops, where crafters make things the way they did one hundred years ago. You can eat barbecued ribs cooked over an open pit and enjoy the evening variety show for $7.95; it promises to be over by 7:00 P.M., so you can make the evening shows at the nearby theaters. Admission is $4.95; children four to eleven, $2.85.

Needless to say, there are many motels around Branson. You can escape the motel rut with a bed and breakfast if you plan ahead a little. Plus, the people in the B&Bs tend to know their way around the town and can give you the shortest, fastest routes to wherever you are planning to go. Call Ozark Mountain Country Bed and Breakfast Service at (800) 695-1546 and let Kay Cameron find you one of the more than thirty-five B&Bs in the Tri-Lakes area near Table Rock Lake, Lake Taneycomo, Branson, or Silver Dollar City or just across the border in Arkansas. She has about a hundred bed and breakfast inns to direct you to in the Ozarks. Kay also has the number of a ticket service that will deliver tickets to any bed and breakfast inn for you.

The easiest way to reach Branson is from Highway 65, which runs through the east end of town. The West Missouri 76 exit will put you on the strip, where you will watch pedestrians speed by your slowly moving car. Or you can use the back entrance and take Highway 248 to the Shepherd of the Hills Expressway to the west side of town, where things will not be much better. You can reach the Branson/Lakes Area Chamber of Commerce at (900) 884–BRANSON for a guide that lists the shows in town and the ticket office phone numbers. There is a $1.50 per minute charge for that call (average three minutes) and you get a recording to leave your name and address. It is sometimes cheaper to call the visitor information number at (417) 334–4136, but that line is often busy and you can be put on hold for about ten minutes. They have a computerized service listing the hotels and motels with vacant rooms. For show tickets you can call BransonTix, a private company that handles about a dozen theaters, at (800) 888–8497.

Do flea markets interest you? You're in the right place; downtown Branson has five of them. If you don't find something in this lineup, you aren't looking very hard, or you have a good deal more self-discipline than most of us!

◆ **The Branson Scenic Railway,** reminiscent of the passenger train era that ended some thirty years ago, made its first run in 1993. Four trains operate daily from the historic railroad depot at 206 East Main in old downtown Branson. Two of the trains go south past the Hollister depot and into the wilderness of the Ozarks. The unspoiled beauty of this unpopulated land has been inaccessible to sightseers until now. Two trains also travel north to James River at Galena. Right now, however, the trains take whatever track is clear, because it's an active rail line. Most often, it's the southern route. Rides are one hour and forty-five minutes long. The trains feature rebuilt passenger cars with silver-domed vista cars. The wail of the whistle warns the people of Branson that the brightly painted diesel engine is nearing a tunnel, curve, or bridge. It sounds continuously as long as the train is in town. Behind the last passenger car another engine tags along. There is no place to turn around so when the train reaches the end of the line, the other engine comes alive and pulls the train back to Branson. For more information call (417)

334–6110 or (800) 287–2462. The price is $18.50 for adults; $17.50 for persons over fifty-five; $8.75 for children six to twelve; and kids under six travel free. Trains depart the depot from Monday through Saturday at 8:30 A.M., 11:00 A.M., 2:00 P.M. and 4:30 P.M. The last train offers a family special when children under twelve ride free. Food is available on the train, from morning muffins to hoagies for lunch.

The ♦Stone Hill Wine Company (417–334–1897), on Highway 165, 2 blocks south of Highway 76 West, is open Monday through Saturday 8:30 A.M. to 6:00 P.M. and noon to 6:00 P.M. on Sunday for cellar tours and wine tasting. Stone Hill makes mead, which is a honey wine made since ancient times. Couples in England were given a month's supply of mead as a wedding gift. The period in which they drank the wine became known as the "honeymoon" (now there's a piece of information you can surely use somewhere). The gift shop sells sausages and cheese made at the winery. Owners Jim and Betty Held also own the winery in Hermann.

Slow down 2 miles outside of town and turn west on Highway V. There's something here you won't want to miss: the ♦School of the Ozarks (417–334–9961 or 334–6411) in Point Lookout.

It's a college campus, all right, but wait! What's going on here? Everybody looks so...busy. This is a different kind of college—a fully accredited, four-year school where each full-time boarding student works at one of sixty-five campus jobs or industries to pay in part for his or her tuition. It calls itself "the campus that works." The rest is provided through scholarships. The campus fruitcake and jelly kitchen is open during business hours weekdays. Student workers bake some 20,000 fruitcakes a year and produce delicious apple butter and many flavors of jelly.

Students built the college itself—it's a pretty one—and run the Ralph Foster Museum and the Edwards Mill (a working replica of an old-time gristmill) as part of their tuition. If you're hungry while you're here, stop at the student-run Friendship House and Gift Shop. It's an all-you-can-eat smorgasbord where the little ones under five can eat for free—can you pass it up? You can get a mighty prime steak here, they tell us. Friendship House is open between 7:00 A.M. and 7:30 P.M. Monday through Saturday and Sunday until 3:30 P.M.

Peace Cathedral, Highlandville

The campus is beautiful, perched on its hill; don't miss the view from Point Lookout. Stand here at dusk when the bells of the carillon roll out over the mist-shrouded river below, if you want goosebumps up and down your arms. When the sun slides down the sky, that sound of bells on the crisp evening air is unforgettable. Williams Memorial Chapel is a fine place to stop for a moment; the tourist bustle slows to a halt here and there's room to breathe.

This you have to see to believe. ◈**Cathedral Church of the Prince of Peace** is the world's smallest cathedral. Situated in Highlandville, it's 3 miles off Highway 65 and 1,500 yards off Highway 160 (take County Road EE to Highlandville.) It is the cathedral of the very, very small Christ Catholic Church, which claimed the title of "the Catholic Peace Church" in 1965. The beautiful Garden of Saints displays statues of about a dozen saints among the flower beds, with many varieties of geraniums surrounding the Ozark-stone building, which looks like a tiny garage. A 1,500–foot trail meanders through the woods and meadows by the 14 Stations of the Cross. But walk right up there and open the door. Inside is a cathedral—-complete with pews, candles, alter, tabernacle, and prie-dieu. A rich stained-glass window catches the sunlight. Mass is said every morning at 11:00 A.M., and a litany for peace is offered every day. Bishop Karl Pruter is the presiding bishop. Built of native stone, the cathedral is 14 feet by 17 feet and seats a congregation of fifteen; it is mentioned in the *Guinness Book of Records*. The blue onion dome suggests the church's Eastern rite affiliation. Bishop Pruter suggests knocking on the door of the house attached to the church by a covered walkway if you want to talk about the Catholic Peace Church. Call (417) 443–3951.

Just a mile east of Highway 65 on Highway 14, the town of **Ozark** is a haven for antiques buffs. The largest collection is housed at the **Maine Streete Mall,** 1994 Evangel, a warehouse along Highway 65 and home to 108 antiques dealers. There are even antique cars inside. The mall is open seven days a week from 9:00 A.M. to 6:00 P.M. Call (417) 581–2575 for information. You will find a couple dozen more shops—filled with a gazillion items—in the town of Ozark itself. But a trip to Ozark itself will find dozens more shops. This town, 15 miles south of Springfield and near enough to Branson to draw its crowds, is a Mecca for folks who love old stuff.

On the road back to Springfield check out the **Vermillion Factory Outlet** (417–744–2058) in Billings, which features oak and walnut items such as cutting boards, wine racks, and butcher-block tables. There is even a bargain room with scrap boxes for craftspeople and woodworkers. Located on Highway 60 southwest of Springfield, the outlet is open from 9:00 A.M. to 5:00 P.M. seven days a week.

CENTRAL MISSOURI

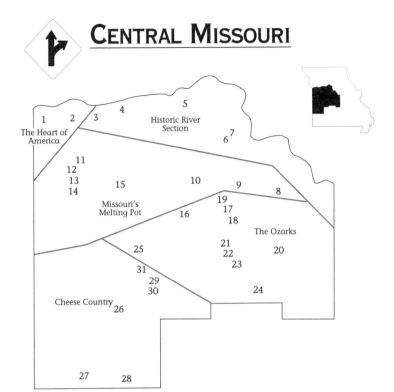

1. Steamboat *Arabia* Museum
2. National Frontiers Trails Center
3. Fort Osage
4. Anderson House State Historic Site
5. Maharishi Kansas City Capital of the Age of Enlightenment
6. Evergreen Restaurant
7. Arrow Rock
8. Burgers' Smokehouse
9. Dutch Bakery and Bulk Food Store
10. Bothwell State Park
11. Powell Gardens
12. Missouri Town 1855
13. Unity Village
14. Greenwood Antiques and Tea Room
15. Contemporary Gallerie
16. Der Essen Platz
17. Lehmans'
18. Pleasant Valley Quilts and Tea Room
19. Shady Oak Market
20. Orr Gallery and Studio
21. Spring Lake Lodge and Antiques
22. Shrine of Mary Mother of the Church
23. Old Trail House
24. Ha Ha Tonka State Park
25. Henry County Museum
26. Carl's Gun Shop
27. Harry S Truman's Birthplace
28. Golden Prairie
29. Osceola Cheese Shop
30. Colby's Cafe
31. The Trunk Shop

Welcome to America's Heartland, where the Mighty Mo marks the end of the glaciated plains, and hill country begins. Remnant prairies tucked between the hills remind us that once these seas of grass covered a third of the state. In this area there are not one but three big lakes, and from Kansas City to the Lake of the Ozarks lie tiny towns built on gentle ridges, waiting to be discovered. Rough gravel roads wind through dogwood forests, along tentacled lakeshores and into towns that seem to have been protected from the rush like the wild morel hidden under a leaf. The big city here is Kansas City: the birthplace of jazz, the homeland of barbecue, and the Heart of America.

Lake of the Ozarks is not only a tourist area, it is a second home site for people from both Kansas City and St. Louis. The eastern shore, known as the St. Louis side, has million-dollar homes in the Land of the Four Seasons Resort area. Six Mile Cove (the six-mile marker means you are six miles from Bagnell Dam) is called Millionaires' Cove by boaters and has some of the most opulent homes in the Midwest. A houseboat business has sprung up on that side, and visitors can now cruise the lake and see both shores without the long drive around the lake.

THE HEART OF AMERICA

Describing Kansas City as a city with "manure on its feet and wheat in its jeans" was a fair assessment at one time. Its two major industries were meat and wheat—all because a man named Joe McCoy convinced the local powers-that-were in 1871 that the newfangled "bobwire" (barbed wire) made it impossible to herd Texas cattle east. A central shipping point was needed, and the Kansas City stockyard was born (where a fine steakhouse, the Golden Ox, is within sniffing distance at 1600 Genessee).

Kansas City is known as the "Heart of America," not because of its location in the center of the country, but because of the people who call it home. Kansas City has a symphony, a lyric opera, the Missouri State Ballet Company, baseball's Royals, and football's Kansas City Chiefs. Enclosed in the very heart of the city is Swope Park, the second-largest city park in the nation, with quiet, tree-shaded picnic areas and a modern zoo on the way to being upgraded to world-class. If you haven't been to KC lately, be sure to drive by the new futuristic Bartle Hall sculptures at night. They are beautiful in a strange space-age way.

The Nelson-Atkins Museum owns one of the finest collections of Oriental art in the world and has a beautiful outdoor sculpture garden. The Kansas City Museum has a planetarium and an old-fashioned ice-cream parlor where you can order a phosphate or a sundae. The Kansas City studio of artist Thomas Hart Benton is now a state park.

Of course, Country Club Plaza, the country's first shopping center, is a must see place if you are from out of town. This is particularly true at Christmastime when each building is intricately outlined in colored lights. The new Brush Creek renovation is also worth a trip if you haven't been here in a while. There are walkways and gardens and even a fountain in the middle of the creek.

The first question most visitors ask when they get off a plane at the Kansas City International Airport is, "Where's the best barbecue?" That's for you to judge: The oldest contenders are **Rosedale Barbecue** at 632 Southwest Boulevard, **Arthur Bryant Barbecue** at 1727 Brooklyn, and **Gates and Sons Bar-B-Q** at 1411 Swope Parkway. All offer carryout, so you can do comparison tests until you are all "pigged out." They all have great meat, but their sauces differ and range from sweet to spicy.

Here and there, drowsing on old streets, pocketed in small shopping centers, crouching behind buildings, or even tucked inside buildings, you're likely to find places that definitely qualify as out of the mainstream. After barbecue, Kansas City is famous for jazz. **The Mutual Musicians' Foundation** is at 1825 Highland Avenue in the old Musicians' Union Hall. Tours are available from 11:00 A.M. until 5:00 P.M. with Dan Cox who will show you around the old hall and share photos of Kansas City in its heyday. But the place really jumps on Friday and Saturday nights when musicians from all over Kansas City gather here to jam. The traditional jazz jam begins when the clubs close at about 1:00 A.M. and lasts until everyone goes home, usually about 3:00 A.M. There is no cover charge, but donations are always welcome to keep this place open. Two big bands play out of the Foundation: The Bennie Motin Orchestra and the Jazz Messengers. Call (816) 471–5212 for information on who is playing where.

Downtown (way downtown), is the **City Market,** where you can shop outdoors with a big wicker basket for just-picked produce in the wonderful atmosphere of a European marketplace. You can buy everything from morel mushrooms in early May to late-harvest turnips in October. There are always fresh eggs and chickens, and on Saturday mornings local farmers and buyers meet over the freshest produce this side of the garden. The area hard by the Missouri River has undergone restoration, complete with a riverboat museum. Rumor has it that now riverboat gambling has been approved by taxpayers and, if millions of dollars in redevelopment money are about to be invested, the area will soon become as busy as it was when Kansas City was young.

The year was 1856 when the steamboat *Arabia* set out for the West, loaded with trade goods and passengers. As the folks at the ◆ **Steamboat *Arabia* Museum** say, you'll find axes, awls, and augers to zillions of other treasures restored to near-mint condition. How did they manage to amass all this in one place? Well, the *Arabia* hit a cottonwood snag in the Missouri River and sank like a stone. There it rested from 1856 to 1988, a time capsule waiting to spill its treasures both everyday and exotic into the present. But of course, even the everyday from over one hundred years ago is exotic now. You'll find spurs, tinware, perfume (that retained its scent after its sojourn under 45 feet of mud and water), wine, whiskey, and champagne (still bubbly), canned goods, hair pins, inkwells, and clothing.

The Hawley family excavated the boat and spent untold hours painstakingly restoring the artifacts they found. To our good fortune, rather than selling off the bounty they opened a museum, and this treasure trove now tells casual visitors, school kids, scholars, living-history reenactors, and just plain history buffs volumes about what life was like on the frontier; civilization was built with the bits and pieces of trade goods carried by packets like the *Arabia*. A short film introduces you to the museum and to the excavation and restoration process. See what frontier life was like for $5.50 for adults, $5.00 for seniors, $3.25 for children four to twelve; younger kids are free. Hours are Tuesday through Saturday, 10:00 A.M. to 6:00 P.M. and Sunday from noon to 5:00 P.M.; for information call (816) 471–4030.

Inside the Fifth Street market building is **Cascone's Grill,** where the market crowd eats. The Cascone family cooks up the most amazing early-morning Italian breakfasts (Italian breaded steak, fried eggs, hash browns, and Italian bread toast) and late-in-the-day lunches featuring Vita Cascone's own spaghetti sauce. They open and close seasonally with the rhythm of the market crowd.

Catty-corner from the market, across the street at 513 Walnut, is **Planters' Seed.** Step inside this old building and inhale the wonderful odors of fresh bulk herbs and spices, the scent of old wood, the aroma of exotic teas and coffees, and the clean smell of seeds. Need a watering can? They've got 'em. Want to buy a pound of dried bay leaves? Look no further. It's a delightful place.

As long as you are in the River Market area, visit **Cheep Antiques River Market Emporium**, 210 Main Street. The store carries furniture in every price range and features antiques from Belgium, France, Germany, England, and Holland. A specialty is making entertainment centers from old armoires. Hours are 9:00 A.M. until 1:00 P.M. Monday through Friday and until 5:00 P.M. on Saturday and Sunday.

The Negro League Baseball Museum is temporarily located at 1601 East Eighteenth Street in the historic Eighteenth and Vine district while its new home is being built. It includes memorabilia of the league that played in the 1920s and 30s before the all-white major leagues would accept black players. Black players formed their own league and some of the best athletes ever to play the game got their start there: players such as Satchel Paige, Ernie Banks, Josh Gibson, and "Cool Papa" Bell. The Kansas City Monarchs were considered the Yankees of black baseball. Blacks were not allowed to play in the majors until 1947 when Jackie Robinson stepped up to bat for the Brooklyn Dodgers. The Negro League was responsible for helping to integrate not only baseball, but America as well. More than 2,600 African-Americans played in the league.

The museum, however, is more than just a collection of pictures and memorabilia. Its centerpiece main gallery recreates the look, sound, and feel of baseball in the heyday of the league. There is a three-station interactive computer module with video games, historical vignettes, and coaching tips. The museum covers the history of the league from its beginning after the Civil War, through its happy ending in the 1960s and features a custom-designed database to search for the play-by-play of league games.

There is a gift shop featuring autographed baseballs, Louisville slugger bats, T-shirts, caps, and jackets.

Baseball League hours are Tuesday through Saturday from 10:00

A.M. to 4:30 P.M., and Sunday from noon to 4:30. Call (816) 221–1920.

Across the street from the Negro League Museum the **Kansas City Jazz Museum** will be completed in late 1996. Kansas City's mayor just bought Charlie "Yardbird" Parker's saxophone to be the first prime exhibit there. His grave site is in Lincoln Cemetery at 8604 Truman Road. The road to the bedraggled cemetery is narrow and unmarked. There is an entrance from Blue Ridge Boulevard.

As long as you are in the area, you might check out a little jazz spot at Nineteenth and Vine. When a Robert Altman movie (aptly named *Kansas City*) was filmed in KC in 1995, the street was restored to its 1930s look complete with fake streetlights. The club's original name, **Mardi Gras,** was used. The owners decided to keep the name. So the sign out front reads either Birdland (the old new name) or Mardi Gras (the new old name). It was in the process of being changed when this book was written. Whatever it is called, there is usually some fine music happening. It's an old jazz club with a young jazz sound. You can enjoy cocktails and dancing until 1:00 A.M.

Black Archives of Mid-America at 2033 Vine Street has documents, artifacts, paintings, and exhibits that explore the lives of African-Americans in Kansas City including musicians, artists, and writers and leaders in many other fields. The first-floor exhibit features the Tuskegee Airmen of World War II, and the second floor is dedicated to the Buffalo soldiers of the Civil War.

The Blue Nile, at 2020 Main Street, is situated in another part of the city that is in transition. This part of Main Street, between busy downtown and Crown Center's upscale neighborhood, is near the old Union Station and slated to become an art district. It was once filled with small hotels and storefront businesses. Daniel Fikro has recently taken one of these small storefronts and is serving the food of his native Ethiopia.

The food is not unusual—an assortment of rich stews and vegetables—but the style of service is. Plan on a casual meal because the food is served as it is in his home country—without silverware of any sort—and it will take a few minutes of practice to get the hang of it. The meats and vegetables are served on a plate lined with a thin spongy bread. Another roll of the same bread (thicker than a tortilla, softer than a pita) accompanies the meal. It is simply a matter of tearing a piece of the rolled bread and using it as a scoop to transport the food from the plate to your mouth without dropping it in your lap. Daniel will show you how to do it easily.

It is worth the effort because the thick sauces surrounding the chicken, beef, or lamb soak into the bread and you will want every drop of it. There is also a large vegetarian selection including lentils, and golden turmeric-flavored steamed cabbage. Ordering the combination platter would be a good choice because it includes your choice of meats and vegetables. But the lamb stew will bring you back to the restaurant again and again.

A lunch buffet is served every day except Sunday from 11:00 A.M. to 2:00 P.M. for the hurried lunch hour crowd, but menu items are always available. Dinner is served from 4:00 to 9:00 P.M. Monday through Thursday and until 10:00 P.M. on Friday. The restaurant is open on Saturday from 11:00 A.M. to 10:00 P.M. and closed on Sunday. Call (816) 472–9090 for more information.

Just south of the busy interstates that ring downtown Kansas City proper is **Central Park Gallery** at 1644 Wyandotte (816–471–7711); it's a newly renovated, 108-year-old, three-story schoolhouse. Brenda and Jim Miles bought the old grade school and converted it into a showcase of Midwestern fine art, highlighting lithographs, raku ware, and original paintings. Hours are 9:00 A.M. to 5:00 P.M. Tuesday through Friday, and from 10:00 A.M. until 4:00 P.M. on Saturday.

Moving south, slow up at the old Union Station. Tucked under the wings of the station is **Creative Candles** (816–474–9711) at 330 West Pershing Road (look sharp or you'll miss it; it's just past the main post office on Pershing—make a hard right and go down below street level). Creative they are indeed. Duane Benton got into the candle business in the sixties like a lot of other idealistic entrepreneurial dropouts; the difference is that Duane kept at it and now sells candles throughout the United States.

Historic Westport, some 40 blocks south of downtown, was the whole city at one time. Some of us think it still is. Check out **The Classic Cup** (816–756–0771) at 4130 Pennsylvania, owned by Charlene Welling. Originally *the* spot in Kansas City for gourmet coffee beans, it now offers a selection of imported cheeses, pâté, and preserves. The bakery, ruled by pastry chef Paul Frazier, offers incredible edibles.

77

The Cup now runneth over; you can pick from one of the finest wine lists in the city and stay for a wonderful lunch. Chef Brenda Sweeny is the creative engine behind the apron. The menu changes daily but is always based on fresh ingredients.

The all-time favorite entree is the raspberry-Dijon mustard sauce on grilled pork tenderloin (sometimes it's blueberry, blackberry, or tart cherry Dijon sauce). Hours are Monday through Thursday from 10:00 A.M. to 10:00 P.M.; Friday and Saturday from 10:00 A.M. to 11:00 P.M.; and Sunday from 11:00 A.M. to 3:30 P.M., including a Sunday brunch from 11:00 A.M. to 2:00 P.M.

The Three Dog Bakery at 612 West 48th Street has tasty-looking cookies arranged in a bakery case. You might be tempted to buy a bagful to munch on as you walk. What you need, however, is a doggie bag, because owners Mark Beckloff and Dan Dye are serving freshly baked treats for your pooch. You can buy your canine a pupcake or a cheese pizza. For the vegetable course there is "collie-flower," and for dessert there are "snicker-poodles," always a favorite. A portion of the price goes to help abused dogs. The treats have no salt or chemicals and are low fat (your dog will thank you). You can also order your loving pet its own specially decorated birthday cake to share with other dogs on the block. Hours are 10:00 A.M. to 7:00 P.M. Monday through Saturday and noon to 5:00 P.M. on Sunday. Call (816) 474–3647 to order that special pal a special cake.

Let's get small. If you love tiny things (or if you haven't quite grown up), don't miss the **Toys and Miniatures Museum** at 5235 Oak Street (816–333–2055). Mary Harris Francis and Barbara Marshall started the museum on a small scale, but its new 14,000-square-foot addition gives them plenty of room for little stuff. There are over eighty-five antique furnished doll-houses at least one hundred years old, scale-model miniature rooms, and boys' toys. The museum is open Wednesday through Saturday 10:00 A.M. to 4:00 P.M. and Sunday from 1:00 to 4:00 P.M. It is closed for two weeks following Labor Day. Admission is $3.00 for adults, and $1.50 for children. There is a puppet show the first Saturday of each month.

Of course, in cities the size of Kansas City there is something for everyone if you know where to look. Sometimes just finding the first place is the key. For example, if your taste leans to designer clothes but your money leans more toward off-the-rack, you might enjoy browsing in some of K.C.'s consignment shops. After pricing new clothes at Country Club Plaza, check out **My Sister's Closet** at 1201 West Forty-seventh Street just 3 blocks west of the Plaza. There sisters Mary Ellison and Michelle Donnelly have a boutique where you will discover Plaza style at much better prices—everything from silk blouses to fur coats. They also have a list of the eleven other consignment shops in the Kansas City area (816–531–0067). Hours are Monday through Friday from 10:00 A.M. until 5:30 P.M. and Saturday until 5:00 P.M.

South of Country Club Plaza, in Brookside, in an old Texaco station, is a small wine bar and cafe called **Joe D's** (6227 Brookside Plaza). It was the first wine bar in the country. Owner Joe DiGiovanni, one of the leaders of *Les Amis du Vin* (Friends of Wine), is a personable young man who will sit down and talk wine anytime.

He has the largest by-the-glass wine list in Kansas City and his house wines are excellent. His menu changes each day, depending on what seasonal fresh produce and meat the chef has discovered. Unusual entrees such as breast of chicken with strawberry peppercorn sauce, orange cream fettucine, or fresh marlin with coconut banana curry sauce are written on a chalkboard. The pizza du jour on fresh Italian Boboli bread (artichoke and crab pizza? Yes!) changes with the chef's mood. Joe D's (816–333–6116) opens weekdays at 11:30 A.M. and serves lunch until 2:30 P.M. Between 2:30 and 5:00 P.M. only appetizers and salads are served; dinner is served after 5:00 P.M. Joe D's closes at 11:00 P.M. on Monday and Tuesday, midnight on Wednesday and Thursday, and 1:00 A.M on Friday and Saturday. After dinner be sure to try the bread pudding with hot caramel sauce, just like grandma used to make. Entrees range from about $8.00 to $18.00.

The city of Independence, just east of downtown Kansas City on Interstate 70, could be a day trip in itself: There's Harry S Truman's home, now a national park, and the **Truman Presidential Library**; the world center for the Reorganized Church of Latter-Day Saints and the RLDS Auditorium; and Civil War battlefields. Here you'll find the beginnings of the Santa Fe Trail, still visible in the worn earth. (Sometimes it seems as if half the towns on this side of the state claim the trail, but in Independence they still celebrate the Santa-Cali-Gon, where the Santa Fe, California, and Oregon trails jumped off into the wilderness.) The recently opened National Frontier Trails Center is a fine place to learn more about the hardships and adventures of those who dared to leave civilization behind and strike out across the wilderness to a new life. It's in the historic Waggoner-Gates Milling Company building. Call (816) 254–0059 for further information.

There are antiques stores, B&Bs, and dandy places to eat—in short, there's entirely too much to include in a single volume. We've narrowed it down to these few, which are off the beaten path by virtue of location, arcane historical significance, or ambience.

Don't miss **Clinton's** on the square, at 100 West Maple. When he was on the campaign train in Independence, President Bill Clinton visited here; they have photos and a thank-you letter to prove it! (He has a Clinton's sweatshirt.) Just how long has it been since you've had a real chocolate soda or cherry phosphate? While you're there, ask them to make a chocolate-cherry cola; it's like a liquid, chocolate-covered cherry with a twist. This is a real old-time soda fountain, complete with uniformed soda jerks and a marble counter with a mirrored back; the malts still whir in those tall, frosty metal containers as they did when we were kids. Call (816) 813-2625 for more information. Clinton's is open daily.

And if all this hedonistic revelry doesn't get you, maybe the historical angle will: Truman's very first job was at Clinton's. You don't have to be a soda jerk first to be President, but maybe it helps. Harry was one of our most popular commanders-in-chief.

You think celebrity prisoners in our jails are pampered now. When Frank James was held at the jail in Independence, his cell sported an Oriental carpet; he had guests in for dinner and served them fine wines. For that matter, so did William Quantrill when he was incarcerated here.

Although the dank cells with their monolithic stone walls were decorated when company called, they were still jail. A hundred and thirty years after the fact, the cells are still dark, forbidding holes that look impossible to escape. **The Old Jail Museum and Marshall's Home** (816–252–1892) are at 217 North Main.

Several interesting B&Bs are in Independence. **Serendipity Bed & Breakfast** at 116 South Pleasant Street is a step back in time. This three-story, 1887 brick house is full of Victorian details. An authentic-looking iron stove hides an electric range, and tall glass-door cabinets are full of antique food containers and plates.

Even the brick-edged flower beds in the garden are alive with color from spring through fall. The most modern item is the 1924 Studebaker in the carriage house, which is driven to take guests on a tour of Independence. Rates are $70, which includes a full breakfast in the dining room. If there are five or more in your party, you can arrange for a Victorian Tour and Tea for $12.50 a person. Call Susan for more information, (816–833–4719).

Perhaps you remember the nineteenth-century painting of two trappers in a long wooden canoe. A big black animal—perhaps a bear—sits in the bow gazing enigmatically at the viewer. Or maybe "The Jolly Boatmen" is more your style, with the rivermen dancing at the dock, playing instruments, and generally raising a ruckus. Artist George Caleb Bingham painted both, along with many others depicting life along the Western Frontier.

Bingham made his home for a time at the elegant **Bingham-Waggoner Estate** at 313 West Pacific, where he watched two Civil War battles rage across his front lawn (not conducive to painting a decent picture. Think what that would do to your concentration!).

Visit from April to October, Monday through Saturday from 10:00 A.M. till 4:00 P.M. to find out how "the other half" lived in the last century—or rent the mansion for a festive event and make the past your own. The mansion is also open from late November through December for the Christmas season; they decorate all twenty-six rooms. Fee is $2.50 for adults, $2.00 for senior citizens, and 50 cents for children under twelve, with slightly higher winter fees to defray the cost of all those decorations. Call (816) 461–3491 for more information.

There is great antiques shopping in this region. Independence was the jumping-off point for pioneers heading west, so this is as far as a lot of their furniture got. Shlepping across the country with a wagon full of sideboards and armoires didn't seem practical, so Independence is where many pioneers began jettisoning large pieces of furniture. (Rocking chairs often made it as far as the Platte River.)

❖**National Frontiers Trails Center** exhibits commemorate the Santa Fe, California, and Oregon trails all of which passed through or began in Independence. The Trails Center doesn't feel like a museum, because it presents the trails through the words of the pioneers who traveled them. The layout of the center is patterned after the trails. At one point, a fork in the path forces visitors to choose between taking the Santa Fe or the Oregon-California routes. One route dead ends, so if you choose that route, you have to go back and try again. Voice-activated boxes tell stories of how the West was settled, and the murals by Charles Goslin show how it was accomplished. There are many pioneers' journals which make fascinating reading, and there is a theater with a trails film. The center is located at 318 West Pacific Street. Call (816) 325–7575 for hours.

The Woodstock Inn Bed and Breakfast at 1212 West Lexington (816-833-2233) offers comfort, privacy, and hospitality. Each of the eleven guest rooms has its own private bath. Rates are from $45 to $70. If you are traveling with a family, try the suite with a queen-size bed and an extra sitting room that can sleep four comfortably for $70.

A maze of interstates has left old Highway 40 very nearly off the beaten path. Find the highway just south of the intersection of Noland Road and Interstate 70, and turn east to **Stevenson's Apple Orchard and Restaurant** at Lee's Summit Road; this one is well worth a stop, as happy eaters from presidents to movie stars have discovered. A large barrel of their famous cider keeps waiting diners happy. Stevenson's is sprawling but done in small rooms to keep the feeling intimate; some rooms are elegant, others are like dining in a rustic wine cellar. Enjoy an apple daiquiri (or peach or strawberry in season) and their famous smoked chicken. Meals are served with almost too many choices (savory green rice, frozen fruit salad, several types of muffins, and Stevenson's own apple fritters). Call (816) 373–5400 for reservations.

And two blocks east of Stevenson's is one of the dandiest antiques malls you'll ever want to explore—**Country Meadows** (816-373-0410), at 4621 Schrank Drive (don't worry, you can see it from Highway 40). It's huge, upstairs and downstairs; plan on taking plenty of time. More than 200 dealers show off their wares in 40,000 square feet of space.

An antiques mall is an antiques mall is an antiques mall, right? Not in this case. There's also a tearoom, if you get hungry; if a powerful thirst is upon you and you just need a treat, there's an old-fashioned soda fountain adjacent to the tearoom.

Exclusively Missouri is Donna Leker's shop inside the mall, offering gifts from all over the state of Missouri, from herbs to

82

quilts to figurines to good old hard candies; if you have a special Missouri need, call her at (816) 373–5767.

For heaven's sake, don't leave town without visiting **The Angel Lady** at 216 South Spring Street (on the southwest corner of the route around the square). Owner Carolyn Pratt has thousands of angels, in this four-room brick gift shop. More than 2,000 seraphim, cherubim, and their brethren—ranging in price from $1.00 to $500.00—fill her little shop just south of the square. Glass angels hang from the windows and reflect the sunlight; golden angels glimmer on tables; pictures of angels hang on the walls. There is a wonderful stained glass window with an angel that Carolyn rescued from an old church and destruction. The shop is open Monday through Saturday. Call for hours (816) 252–5300.

Every town tries to have the weirdest little museum and the **Hair Museum** gives Independence a lock on that title. (Ow! sorry.) You can see a 14-inch high tree made of human hair. There are more than 700 pieces of jewelry and pictures all made from hair and dating before 1900. The Hair Museum is at 815 West 23rd Street. There is a $3.00 admission charge. Call (816) 252–HAIR for more information.

Independence is the center of the Reorganized Church of Jesus Christ of Latter-Day Saints, and the new temple is something to behold. But at the old RLDS auditorium, the one with the green dome at 1001 West Walnut, you can take your children to the non-denominational Children's Peace Pavilion. There they can play games that help them learn co-operation, communication, and self-esteem, and have a good time. The peace pavilion is on the fourth floor; admission is free. Call (816) 521–3033 for information.

HISTORIC RIVER SECTION

How about a day trip back in time? It's 1803, the year of the Louisiana Purchase: Imagine Missouri nearly empty of "civilization," as it was when it became part of the United States. Early fur trappers traded necessities—like tobacco, tomahawks, blankets, fabrics, and cookware. The Osage peoples were the most common Indians in this area, and they did business amicably with both French and American trading posts.

East of Independence you'll explore ◆ **Fort Osage,** a National Historic Landmark and the westernmost U.S. outpost in the

Louisiana Purchase; its site was chosen by Lewis and Clark; construction was originally supervised by William Clark himself. Strategically overlooking the Missouri River, the fort was reconstructed from detailed plans preserved by the U.S. War Department. The factory building stands today on its original foundation. Artifacts unearthed during the excavation are on display in the visitors' center.

You may find a living history reenactment in progress, complete with trappers and military men, Indians, explorers, storytellers, and musicians. Clothing displayed is authenticated down to the last bit of trim, and guides learn their alter egos' life and times so thoroughly that you forget you are only visiting the past. Sit inside the blockhouse looking out at the river, watch arrowheads being made from local flint, or visit the gift shop to purchase unique items with a sense of history (like real bone buttons).

Rustle up a group to enjoy one of the after-hours programs offered by Jackson County Heritage Program. You can reserve a place at a hearthside supper in the factory's dining rooms for example. Enjoy an authentic nineteenth-century meal by candlelight; then cozy up to the fireplace and savor the entertainment.

Several weekends a year, special events such as the Sheep Shearing (May), or Militia Muster and Candlelight Tour (October) are offered, or spend the Fourth of July as our forebears did—the fort's a great place for it.

To find Fort Osage (816–249–5737), take Highway 24 from Kansas City east to Buckner; turn north at Sibley Street (Highway BB); follow the gray signs through the tiny town of Sibley. Special weekend activities are 9:00 A.M. to 4:30 P.M. You can explore on your own Wednesday through Sunday from April till November. Admission is $3.00 for adults and $1.00 for senior citizens and children ages five through thirteen. Children four or under are free.

A more historic (and scenic) route between Fort Osage and Lexington will take you down the Highway 224 spur through Napoleon, Waterloo, and Wellington. This is Lafayette County —beginning to get the picture here? Must have been history buffs around this area since dirt was young. The road runs along the Missouri River, sometimes almost at water level, other times from a spectacular river-bluff view.

Don't miss the turnoff to tiny downtown Napoleon; it's a

Fort Osage, Sibley

lovely place to pick up a bit of lunch in a real old-fashioned general store. The **G&S General Store** celebrated its centennial in 1992. This is no upscale yuppie fern bar; you'll find hardware, horse liniment, and canned goods on the aisles leading back to the deli area. And what a deli—it's an old-time meat case where owners will make you a sandwich while you wait—maybe a fresh pink pastrami on rye with the works. A big case full of soft drinks, milk, and juices completes the offerings.

Across the street is **Ma & Pa's Riverview Antiques Mall** (816–934–2698), and a wonderful view. The Missouri River shines like a mirror far below, and rich bottomland fields fill the rest of the space to the far hills. Vicki Merritt welcomes you Monday through Saturday 9:30 A.M. to 5:00 P.M. and Sunday from noon to 5:00 P.M.

A bit farther on is Waterloo, just between Napoleon and Wellington—the obvious place, don't you think? There's not much here but a sign and a few houses, but it would be perfect even if it were only the sign!

On the way into Lexington, watch for colorful sights guaranteed to make you smile, like the A-frame wedding chapel overlooking the river, the old Peckerwood Club, and a grain silo painted to look like a lighthouse—and that glorious old river.

Once you enter historic Lexington, soak up the antebellum ambience. The homes along Highway 24 and on South Street are wonderful examples of Victorian charm—and, remember, we're not just talking 1890s gingerbread here. The Victorian era began in the 1840s. You'll itch to get inside some of these beauties; check with the chamber of commerce for dates and times on historic homes tours. Lexington has four national historic districts and 110 antebellum and Victorian homes and shops. There are several good B&Bs, too.

The **Edwards Home Bed and Breakfast,** 1601 Franklin Street, is owned by Marilou and John Edwards. The Greek revival farmhouse was built in the 1830s. The single guest room has a private bath. It was the first B&B in Lexington. Out back, there is an English cottage garden with a fish pond and flowers. Marilou is the director of the 1830s Log House and loves to share historical anecdotes with her guests. Guest room costs $50 a night. Call (816) 259–6375 for information.

Linwood Lawn is a Southern antebellum home on the National Register. Resembling an Italianate mansion, it boasts 14-foot ceilings, seven marble fireplaces, a hand-carved walnut staircase and ornate English chandeliers. Owner Wes Fisher and manager Paul Baswell cook up specialties such as Italian waffles or French omelets with bacon or ham. For $4.00, you can tour the home by appointment any day if you are just passing through. Rooms cost from $75 to $95 and dinner is about $35. Go one mile southeast of Highway 24 on County Road 107 to reach Linwood Lawn.

The area around the courthouse has plenty of places to browse in. Probably the neatest place in town is the **Victorian Peddler Antiques Shop and Tea Room** at 900 Main Street. Rebecca Hooser and her daughter Melissa Clark carry fine Victorian furniture but you can also have lunch there. The tearoom has an eclectic assortment of antique tables and chairs. As Rebecca says, "if you like your table, you can take it home with you." The menu changes each day, but there is always a quiche, a soup and gourmet sandwich available to eat before you order a piece of homemade pie. Everything is made from scratch. Hours are Tuesday through Saturday from 10:00 A.M. until 5:00 P.M., and Sunday from noon to 4:00 P.M. The tearoom, however, is closed on Sunday. Call (816) 259–4533 for more information. Walk around Lexington after lunch and visit the new **Bit of Whimsy Antiques Shop** across the street. The shop is open Monday and Thursday through Saturday 10:00 A.M. to 5:00 P.M., Sunday noon to 5:00 P.M.; and closed Tuesday and Wednesday. For more information call (816) 259–6531.

About a block away, the **Monument Antiques Shop** at 901 Franklin is also interesting to visit. You will recognize it by the large stone monument by the front door.

Ma & Pa's Bakin' Place (816–259–6612) is a little farther down the block at 929 Main. This place is full of cookies, cakes, potato and salt-rising bread, and other freshly baked treats, and it opens at 6:00 A.M. every day except Sunday, so you can stop in before you hit the road. James Covey and the aptly named Karen Baker are the owners; these game young people have been known to attend local fairs in period costume, baking their delights outdoors in an old-fashioned woodstove.

Be sure to stop by the restored **Log House Museum** at 307 Broadway. This 1830s home was discovered in a rundown condition and was moved and rebuilt log by log by the volunteer efforts of local citizens. Now it is surrounded by wildflowers and paths as it might have been when it was new. Spinning wheels, quilts, and other items of the era fill the little cabin, and a gift shop is in the back; admission is $2.00 for adults and $1.00 for children under twelve. Hours are Wednesday through Saturday 11:00 A.M. to 4:00 P.M. and Sunday noon to 4:00 P.M. From November to April, however, the house is open only by appointment; it's too expensive to keep it warm through the winter months on a day-to-day basis. Call the log house at (816) 259–4711 during open hours. The Battle of Lexington was fought in September 1861 when General Sterling Price moved his Confederate troops north after the Battle of Wilson's Creek and the fall of Springfield. After fifty-two hours of fighting, Union troops surrendered to the invaders. General Price took 3,000 prisoners and broke the chain of Union-held posts along the Missouri River. Remnants of the battle endure; a cannonball remains lodged in a pillar of the courthouse. You can still find earthworks out behind ◆**Anderson House State Historic Site** (816–259–2112) overlooking the Missouri River. This red-brick house served as headquarters and hospital for both sides and is now a Civil War museum.

Along Highway 24 toward Waverly, the land undergoes a change from fenced, row-cropped fields to orchards. The peach crop is always at risk in Missouri's unpredictable weather. Blossoms are often teased out early by a mild February to be punished by an April freeze. It is a dangerous business, but the area around Waverly perseveres. The best peaches from this area are huge and sweet and dripping with juice. A bad year for the peach business is when the fruit is too big, too juicy, and not nearly plentiful enough to make shipping profitable. This is bad for orchard owners but wonderful for anyone lucky enough to be driving through.

Highway 24 is the old Lewis and Clark Trail along the river. Now it is filled with markets where orchard owners sell their bounty to travelers. Pick up peaches and apples or honey, home-made sausages, cheese, and cider—along this scenic drive.

◆**The Maharishi Kansas City Capital of the Age of Enlightenment,** believe it or not, is on Highway 24 near Waverly. There Joanne Grigas and her staff manage an elegant seventy-five-room residence-course facility on 260 forested acres, covered with walking trails, wildlife, and a fountain. The house can be home to as many as forty-five people—mostly businesspeople, doctors, and lawyers from the Kansas City area—who practice transcendental meditation, or "TM." (There are over a thousand names on the mailing list; as many as 5,000 people who practice TM in the Kansas City area.) The clinic is a Maharishi Ayur-Veda health education center for those already involved in the discipline of TM. A weekend in this magnificent estate, with its three gold domes, and an advanced course in TM costs $110 a day, which includes a uniquely decorated room, instruction, and vegetarian meals. Call JoAnne (816–493–2285) for more information about the programs offered at the center.

The Santa Fe Trail ran through here at one time, and it is still a trail of sorts for people living in the area: It is Missouri's apple and peach country. The Santa Fe Trail Growers Association is made up of seventeen members in the area. On a drive along

Highway 24 you will see a bountiful expanse of apples, peaches, nectarines, strawberries, raspberries, and blackberries—and all for sale if the season is right. Schreiman and Burkhart are just a few of the orchards you will pass along the road. Greenhouses along the way are filled with vegetables, sweet corn, cider, and honey. In July, **Peters Market** is worth the drive from Kansas City for many people.

About a mile outside the town of Arrow Rock on Highway 41 stands a comfortable white Victorian house shaded by old trees. It is now the home of Bob and Chris Rappold's ◆ **Evergreen Restaurant** (816–837–3251), a good spot to have a quiet dinner during the season at Arrow Rock's Lyceum Theater. Warm antiques and a fireplace in every room create a cozy ambience in which to enjoy really fine country cooking. Chris's Chocolate Mousse Cake is a sinful way to finish a meal; if you want to feel more virtuous, order the seasonal fruit tart. Evergreen closes after Christmas and opens again in the spring.

Bob and Chris are new owners of the Evergreen; they were proprietors of Cafe Europa in Columbia. If it's any indication of how good their food is, former happy customers drive all the way from Columbia to find them at their new location, where they've kept some of the old Evergreen's recipes while adding favorites from Cafe Europa.

On matinee days—Wednesdays and Saturdays—during the theater season, hours are 11:30 A.M. to 3:00 P.M. for lunch, and 5:30 to 8:30 P.M. for dinner, and 4:00 to 7:00 P.M. on Sundays. In the winter Evergreen is open Friday, Saturday, and Sunday. If you have a group and let Bob know ahead of time, they'll open any time for private parties. Historical gossip is that Jesse James once hid upstairs; listen quietly and you may hear his ghost. The Rappolds' emphasize the importance of having reservations because the location of the Evergreen is so far off the beaten path that finding extra help for unexpected crowds is impossible.

Pioneers stopped at historic ◆ **Arrow Rock** on their way west; it was a Santa Fe Trail town, a river port, and a meeting place for those who shaped history. More than forty original buildings remain. Arrow Rock is still a real town, with permanent residents, a grocery store, a gas station, and a post office, but it is also a state park and historic site. The population is only 70 (and the historic district so tightly controlled that someone has to die before someone new can move in, they say) but the place is packed in the summertime when the Lyceum Theatre is active. The state leases out the Old Tavern Inn; and it draws people from all over the state. Fried chicken, ham, blueberry cobbler and wonderful bread pudding make people come back again and again. There is more, too. The 160-year-old tavern (that word was synonymous with hotel then) was home to travelers on the Santa Fe Trail or people bound for Independence and the Oregon Trail. Some died here of the cholera and typhus that stopped the westward trek of many. And so, the place is haunted. Beds used in exhibits on the second floor have been found mussed, quiet voices have been heard as well as the cries of a child whose mother died here; photos show strange images that are not really there and once, a mysterious cloud of smoke appeared in the manager's upstairs bedroom. They seem to be friendly spirits, though. Dinners are bounteous and amazingly inexpensive ($10.95 will buy a huge meal, from salad to dessert). The museum is upstairs.

Arrow Rock looks like a normal town, but normal for a hundred years ago. Streets and gutters are made from huge blocks of limestone; board sidewalks clatter with footsteps. The old bank acts as ticket office for the Lyceum, and the tiny stone jail still waits for an inmate. You may camp at Arrow Rock State Park; sites are available for groups or individuals.

Today, the **Lyceum Repertory Theatre** (816–837–3311) offers performances throughout the summer in an old church building; it's Missouri's oldest repertory company. Call ahead for a list of plays and their rotating dates.

Borgman's Bed and Breakfast (816–837–3350) is a nineteenth-century inn with five bedrooms and a common game room. Play a quick round of Scrabble, or enjoy a fireside chat with the Borgmans. Mother-and-daughter team Helen and Kathy Borgman did much of the restoration work themselves; take a look at the fascinating "house book," which shows step-by-step what's been done. Helen will fix you a generous breakfast, and Kathy will give you a tour of the town—she's an official Arrow Rock guide. Additional meals are available if you make prior arrangements. A cat and bird are in residence, so no other pets are welcomed. Rates are $45.50 for a double. (Next door to Borgman's is Keelor Handweaving, where you can buy yourself a warm, luxurious treat.)

Artist George Caleb Bingham's home is here (remember him from Independence?), as is the home of Dr. John Sappington, one of the first to use quinine to treat malaria; Kathy Borgman will tell you all about it.

River Country Bed and Breakfast Service represents several B&Bs in Arrow Rock. Call (314) 771–1993 for information.

One and a half miles west of Arrow Rock on Highway TT Chuck and Jeanie Holland have a restored antebellum country home with three rooms furnished in period antiques (one downstairs with private bath) waiting for you at the **Airey Hill Bed and Breakfast.** A full country breakfast of ham and eggs, quiche with homemade muffins, or pancakes greets you each morning. Rooms have double beds and are $45 a night. The home is "out in the country" according to Jeanie, so call (816) 886–5815 for reservations.

At **Boonville,** following the river east, the western prairie meets the Ozarks. The town was settled in 1810 by the widow Hannah Cole, who, with her nine children, built cabins on the bluffs overlooking the Missouri River. During the War of 1812 the settlement was palisaded and named Cole's Fort. It became the main river port for all of southwestern Missouri.

The older residential section of Boonville has an unusually well preserved collection of antebellum brick residences with wide halls and large rooms. Modest neoclassical homes are mixed with more flamboyant Victorian ones; many are on the National Register of Historic Places.

While in Boonville visit the **Old Cooper County Jail and Hanging Barn** at 614 East Morgan. The jail was built in 1848 and used until 1978 when public hanging was declared cruel and unusual punishment. Prisoners' quarters resemble dungeons, where the inmates were sometimes shackled to the wall with metal rings. Outside the jail is the hanging barn where nineteen-year-old Lawrence Mabry was executed in 1930, the state's last public hanging (as told in historian Bob Dyer's folk song, "The Last Man to Hang in Missouri").

Thespian Hall is the oldest theater still in use west of the Alleghenies. Originally built in 1857, it has been used as an army barracks, Civil War hospital, and skating rink, among other things. It has featured gymnastics, opera, and movies in its day and is now the home of the Boonville Community Theatre.

If you are out walking around, search out Harley Park, where Lookout Point sits atop a bluff over the Missouri River, and get a feel for what early townsfolk saw along the long bend of the river. An Indian burial mound surmounts this high point; imagine the prospect of immortality with such a view.

The mid-Missouri area was the site of many of the key battles of the Civil War. The first land battle of the war was fought 4 miles below Boonville on June 17, 1861. State troops under the command of Confederate Colonel John S. Marmaduke were defeated by federal forces led by Captain Nathaniel Lyon. Military historians consider this victory important in preserving the Union.

Jefferson City, Missouri's capital, is smack in the center of the state on Highway 50, handy to legislators and lobbyists. Built on the steep southern bluffs of the Missouri River, the city and the surrounding rural landscape offer considerable scenic variety. Large streams are bordered with steeply sloping and heavily forested hills. Bottomland here is rich with alluvial and yellow loess soils that don't look the way you expect fertile topsoil to look but support more wheat and corn than any other section of the Ozarks.

Here also is Jefferson Landing, one of the busiest centers of the nineteenth century. It's still busy; the Amtrak station is at the landing, as are the Lohman Building, the Union Hotel, and the Maus House.

The State Capitol is certainly on the path; however, once inside the House Lounge, you will find a mural painted in 1935 by Thomas Hart Benton. This mural stirred controversy in 1936 because some of the legislators said it lacked refinement. Always quick with an answer, Benton retorted that he portrayed "people involved in their natural, daily activities that did not require being polite."

MISSOURI'S MELTING POT

Head west to California (that's California, Missouri) on Highway 50 and ✦ **Burgers' Smokehouse** if you fancy a ham to carry home. It is open from 7:30 A.M. to 5:00 P.M., 3 miles south of California on Highway 87 (just follow the signs). This family-owned smokehouse has been in business for the past twenty-five years and is one of the largest country meat-processing plants in the United States, producing 200,000 hams annually. You can take a tour of the plant any day but Sunday between 7:30 A.M. and 4:00 P.M. Now there is a toll-free number for ordering a ham: (800) 624–5426. Call (314) 796–4111 for information if you are in the area.

What you wouldn't expect to find here are the seasonal dioramas, which show the beauty of the Ozarks with great care for botanical and zoological detail. These scenes by artist Terry Chase depict the influence of Ozark geography and changing seasons on the process of curing meat.

If you feel in the gallery mood—or just in the mood for a fascinating chat with a man who always has time to sit down and have a cup of coffee—check out **Beryl White's Studio and Gallery** at 401 North High Street (314–796–2303). Beryl has been restoring this old Victorian storefront building for some time; it is now on the National Register. It's just the place if you're running short of sketching supplies while dawdling off the path. Beryl stocks everything from books to brushes and offers oil painting classes as well.

Memory Lane Bed and Breakfast is also in California. This 1896 Victorian is filled with antiques and is next door to an antiques shop, too. The three guest rooms have double beds and twin beds and all share a hall bath. The room rate of $35 includes a hearty breakfast. Call Ozark Mountain Country Reservation Service at (800) 695–1546 for more information.

Highway 50 will take you to the town of Tipton. Follow the signs to the ❖ **Dutch Bakery and Bulk Food Store** (816–433–2865). Located on highways 5 and 50 at the west end of Tipton, the shop is owned by Leonard and Suetta Hoover. Suetta does all the baking right here in the house while minding their six children and seems unruffled by it all. Old Order Mennonites, they came here from Pennsylvania and speak Pennsylvania Dutch when alone in the shop or talking to the children. Her pies are baked from home-grown berries and fruit; fresh vegetables from their garden are available in season. Homemade breads (a favorite is a wonderful oatmeal bread) and rolls fill shelves along with bulk foods. But the primary reason for stopping here is the "Dutch letters"—crisp, thick pastry rolled and filled with almond paste and shaped into letters. They are cheaper if you buy five, and you might as well so you won't have to turn around and come back in an hour.

At the intersection of highways 50 and 65 in Sedalia is an old-fashioned fifties drive-in called the **Wheel Inn.** You must try their Guberburger; a hamburger grilled with peanut butter and served with mayonnaise, tomato, lettuce, and pickles. Before you shout *"Yuck!"* try it. They are deadly good and habit forming. *Note:* The Wheel Inn is closed on Tuesdays.

If you're in the mood for some really good barbecue, however, turn south on Highway 65 at that intersection and drive to 1915 South Limit to **Kehde's Barbecue** (816-826-2267), where John and Chelsea Kehde (pronounced K.D.) serve the best barbecue in the area. But that's not all, Kehde's also has jalapeño fries (french fries dipped in some kind of spicy coating) and a grilled tenderloin sandwich that is as good as the fried kind but without all the fat. Kehde's is a regular stop for folks headed to or from the Lake of the Ozarks and Kansas City. Kehde's recently added a railroad dining car to the building to handle the extra crowds from the state fair and summertime Lake of the Ozarks crowd. It's fun to sit up in the old dining car and watch the traffic go by while enjoying the best barbecued ribs in the area. Take home a bottle of the sauce. In fact, take a couple or you will have to send for more when you get home.

If you drive into Sedalia on Highway 65, you will probably pass (off to your left and way up) a beautiful stone mansion overlooking the highway. It is Stony-ridge Farm in ❖ **Bothwell State Park.** Bothwell chose limestone as his primary building material for the lodge and cliff house. There are more angles to this place than a Chinese puzzle—it must have driven the roofers crazy. The original carriage road rises almost 100 feet but in a gentle ascent, with the lay of the land; hand-laid stone culverts allow water passage under the road. Take the first left after you pass the house on Highway 65 going toward Sedalia (or, driving north, watch very carefully for the small sign marking the turn, or you will have to turn around and go back when you finally see it). It is worth the trouble to find; there are spectacular views and wonderful walking trails near the house.

Also in Sedalia is the **Sedalia House** (816–826–6615). Innkeeper Dan Ice welcomes guests to his elegantly furnished, two-story colonial home. The surrounding countryside is beautiful year-round. This is a 300-acre working farm that includes a creek and woods. Deer and turkey hunting are available in season, and

Bothwell State Park, Sedalia

rooms include a full breakfast. Rates are $48 and up to $55 with private bath.

There are several antiques malls in Sedalia, but remember that in August this is the home of the Missouri State Fair, which attracts more than 300,000 people. The path gets beaten smooth, but it leads to midway rides, big-name entertainment, livestock shows, and car races—good, clean, all-American fun. To make your life a little easier, call River Country Bed and Breakfast Service at 314-771-1993 ahead of time and reserve a room in one of the many B&Bs in Sedalia.

The KATY Trail snakes along the river for 83 miles from Sedalia east to Jefferson City, burrowing through its only tunnel at Recuperate. The trail also treats you to the only Missouri River railroad bridge near Franklin and past glittering Burlington limestone bluffs containing millions of fossils from the sea. The Mighty Mo has been out of banks twice since the trail was begun, once in the Great Flood of '93 and again in the almost greatflood of '95, but work is progressing to connect the trail here with its other end in St. Charles. When the river is behaving, you can look "across the wide Missouri" and have a magnificent view of the river traffic of barges and boats.

If you continue west on Interstate 70, you will come to Odessa. The town has become a popular destination for the Kansas City crowd, because it has a new factory outlet mall. Sandy and Butch Heinman have opened a new business, too, but in the 86-year-old Olde Stone Church in Oak Grove, which is right on the route from Kansas City to Odessa on Highway 71. **Lamp Lite Antiques and Oddities** is the result of the Heinmans' auction habit, so it will be restocked often. The shop is open seven days a week from 10:00 A.M. until 6:00 P.M. except Tuesdays when closing time is 5:00 P.M. The first floor has antiques, primitives, and collectibles. The lower level has flea market items. Call (816) 690-7797 for information.

Western Missouri waited a long time for a botanical garden; St. Louis, in the east, has one of the finest in the country. Finally, after much hemming and hawing among folks in the Greater Kansas City area and those just over the Kansas border, the people of ◆ **Powell Gardens** couldn't wait any longer and began their own. Hurrah for private initiative! This is a beautiful, not-for-profit, 807-acre garden and natural resource center where you can wander among the flowers and indigenous plants, learn about "S-s-s-s-snakes!," make an all-natural wreath, or learn how to plant, prune, and harvest your own backyard botanical garden—you get the idea. The new chapel at the gardens was designed by E. Fay Jones, a nationally honored and recognized architect who built Thorncrown Chapel in Arkansas. Hours are Tuesday to Friday from 8:00 A.M. to 5:00 P.M. and weekends from 9:00 A.M. to 6:00 P.M. Workshops and seminars are scheduled year-round. Powell Gardens (816-566-2600) is just south of Highway 50 at Kingsville.

Watch for signs from Interstate 70 (or Highway 291) for Fleming Park and Lake Jacomo. You'll find the usual sailing, swimming, and fishing as well as the **Burroughs Audubon Society Library** (816-795-8177). Learn about the birds, take a hike, browse through the books, and discover how to turn your backyard into a wildlife sanctuary. The library is open from noon to 4:30 P.M.

Stop in your tracks. The world is moving altogether too quickly, but there's an antidote: ◆ **Missouri Town 1855** in Fleming Park. Managed by the Jackson County Parks Department, one of the two largest county parks departments in the United States, it's a collection of original mid-nineteenth-century buildings moved on-site. They now make up a brand-new old town founded in 1960.

A wide variety of architectural styles add to the historical significance of the town. It's just that sort of progression from rugged log cabins to fine homes that would have taken place in the last century as settlers arrived and commerce thrived. You'll find antebellum homes, a tavern, a schoolhouse, a church, a lawyer's tiny office (apparently the law was not quite so lucrative then), and the mercantile, where settlers would have bought outright or bartered for their goods. It has even been the setting for several movies, including the television version of *Friendly Persuasion,* and the more recent movie *Across Five Aprils,* a story of a family split by the Civil War.

If the buildings alone aren't enough to pique your interest, this is a "living history" experience. You're liable to see the blacksmith at work, watch oxen tilling the soil, or be followed by the resident flock of geese. You can wander around a real herb garden and discover how many were used as medicinals in the past century—hospitals were rare in those days, and medical insurance was unheard of.

Missouri Town 1855 is on the east side of Fleming Park. Take Colbern Road east to Cyclone School Road. Turn north (left) and follow the signs two miles to the entrance. Admission for adults is $3.00, $1.00 for youths and children under four get in for free. The town is open Wednesday through Sunday from 9:00 A.M. till 5:00 P.M. from April 15 through November 15 and on weekends only from November till April.

Now it is dinnertime, and you are in for a surprise! Find the **Bistro on Main Street** at 235 S.E. Main Street in the historic Strother's District of Lee's Summit. Here Mary and Dan Dannald-son have designed a place where customers feel as if they are eating at an outdoor bistro in France. The original 1887 fir floors and a freight elevator, which sits in the back corner, add a certain charm to this upscale restaurant. *Bistro* is a French word meaning fast. Its use comes from the Russians who were in France for the War of 1812. French bistros have traditionally been in alleys, so Dan has created the feel of being between two buildings, with real doors, windows with awnings, exposed brick, and flowers. The food is simple, yet elegant and beautifully presented; there is an affordable wine list to go along with it. Dinner entrees range from $7.00 to $14.00. Hours are 11:00 A.M. to 2:00 P.M. for lunch and dinner is served from 5:00 until 9:00 P.M. (10:00 P.M. on Friday and Saturday). Next door at 235 S.E. Main Street, Dan has **Strother's,** a neat little 1860s restaurant and microbrewery serving sandwiches and twenty-five microbrew beers on tap. Call (816) 246–0600 for information.

◆ **Unity Village,** on Highway 50 just west of Lee's Summit, is an incorporated town with its own post office and government. It's a peaceful setting with an Old World feel; spacious grounds contain a natural rock bridge, Spanish Mediterranean-style buildings, and a formal rose garden with reflecting pools and fountains. People of all faiths use the resources at Unity. The restaurant, bookstore, and chapel are open to the public, and you may arrange an overnight stay by calling (816) 524–3550.

Little Greenwood is just south of Lee's Summit on Highway 291, then east on Highway 150. This was once a bustling place with not one but two train stations. It was a major shipping center for cattle and lumber. It still has two explosives factories and a rock quarry nearby, accounting for the heavy trucks rumbling through this sleepy town.

An old wooden bridge marks the end of downtown proper; watch for signs to find any number of little antiques stores and factory outlets. ◆ **Greenwood Antiques and Tea Room** at Fifth and Main streets is a mall-type operation hard by the railroad bridge and just full of small booths. More than seventy shops occupy 15,000 square feet of space. The food is excellent; add your name to the waiting list when you go in the door, and they'll find you. Hours are 11:30 A.M. to 3:00 P.M. Monday through Saturday. Call (816) 537–7172 for more information.

This book can't begin to list all of the antiques shops, tearooms, and outlet stores in this town. One of the newest and most beautiful, though, is **The Gatehouse Antiques and Tea Room** one block south of Highway 150 on Allendale Lake Road. Here two floors of primitives, handmade country clothing, collectibles, and antiques share space with a country tearoom. Hours are Tuesday through Saturday 10:00 A.M. to 5:00 P.M. and Sunday from noon until 5:00 P.M. You can get a list of all the antiques shops in Greenwood at your first stop and spend the day checking them out.

Lone Jack is another unlikely spot for an upscale restaurant, but the **Cafe Periwinkle,** at 103 West 50 Highway offers casual yet elegant dining in a new plantation-style home. The menu features such interesting items as French pepper steak in a Parisian pepper sauce, chicken al pesto, and shrimp thermidor. A good wine list complements the menu. The front room is formal, with table linens; the back room is more masculine, a back-from-the-hunt feeling. For private events or for busy nights there are three additional rooms upstairs: the Louis XIV, Flag, and Southwestern. There is even a gift and antiques shop. Call (816) 697–3599 for information. Hours are Tuesday through Saturday from 11:00 A.M. to 2:00 P.M. for lunch and 5:00 to 9:00 P.M. for dinner. Sunday brunch is served from 11:00 A.M. to 4:00 P.M.

Raymore is home to **The Cranberry Hill Gift Shop and Tea Room** at 1268 West Foxwood Drive. Yes, it is just what it sounds like: a *chic* place, not for the macho-man type at all. Pink and white lace cloths on tiny round tables are set with crystal, silver, and linen. It is a gracious place to take a girlfriend to lunch. The cashew chicken salad is a favorite. The tearoom is open from 11:00 A.M. to 2:00 P.M. Tuesday through Saturday.

If you still haven't gotten enough of the War between the States, head south and east of Warrensburg to **Cedarcroft Farm** at 431 Southeast Y Highway, a farm getaway B&B where Bill and Sandra Wayne have an 1867 farmhouse on eighty scenic acres to share with you. Bill is a Civil War reenactor and historian who can tell you a lot about the history of this area. He belongs to a reenactment unit based in Warrensburg that makes living history presentations, joins parades, and works at historic sites. He even has a uniform you can try on and a musket he will teach you to shoot. Sandra turns out a "more-than-you-can-eat" country breakfast accompanied by cookies, fudge, nut bread, and a table full of country cooking. The two guest rooms are decorated with period furniture. The house was built by Sandra's great-grandfather who was a Union soldier. A two-bedroom private suite with two double beds and private baths, a complimentary evening snack, large five-menu breakfast costs $65 (will go up to $75 in 1996) a night for two. They will even pick you up at the Amtrak station. Horseback riding is available, too. For information call (816) 747–5728 or (800) 368–4944. The farmstead is on the Historic Register and dates from the 1860s. The basement barns for the horses are unique because the horses sleep downstairs and the loft is at ground level. This prominent farmstead has what Sandra calls "a little Garden of Eden on the back 40" so consenting adults can walk in the woods, play in the creek and "do some smooching." It's a good place to get away from the kids for the weekend. Sandra will fix you a free dinner if you stay more than two nights. As you might suspect, this B&B fills quickly so call early. Sandra can direct you to the nearby Amish community in Windsor and lots of other interesting places in the area.

Warrensburg is the home of Central Missouri State University. It is a fair-to-middlin'-size city now as it grows with the university. Coming into town on Highway 13 or Highway 50, you may have noticed several life-size animal sculptures made of scrap metal or pieces of wood. These are the handiwork of sculptor Jim Myers. Jim says he has been making scrap-wood sculptures since he was a kid; his dad owned a lumber yard. He studied at the Hollywood Art Center in California and the Paris American Academy in France before returning to open his ✪ **Contemporary Gallerie** (816–429–2107) in 1982, where he displays his smaller wood sculptures and oils.

The **Camel Crossing Bed and Breakfast** at 210 East Gay (816–429–2973) belongs to Joyce and Ed Barnes. It is a lovely turn-of-the-century home in the residential area near the university. Tastefully decorated with Middle Eastern and Oriental accents gathered while the couple lived in Saudi Arabia, the place has a unique flavor, including a collection of several hundred camel figures. A camel crossing sign is used as their logo. Rates are $50, or $65 with private bath.

If you are headed north on Highway 13, there is a little surprise waiting for you about 4 miles north of Warrensburg near Fayetteville. Standing patiently near the highway are Ogbid and his wife Ishtar watching traffic roll by day after day. Ogbid and Ishtar are made of old oil drums, engine pistons, metal buckets, and assorted springs and reflectors, giving them a nightlife of sorts. Their son Nimrod joined them a few years ago. Nimrod resembles his parents, although he is unique because his head is an old metal chamber pot.

Then Cousin It joined the family. He is made from an old water heater with a Freon canister for a head, and he's covered with thousands of yards of baling wire, each strand individually attached. Cousin It, with 150 pounds of hair, looks more like a furry family pet than a relative.

The creator, J.C. Carter, lives up the hill. He's had fun with his

Jim Myers Sculpture, Contemporary Gallerie

hobby of creating "assembled metal sculptures," sort of recycling-gone-bonkers. He has visions when he sees industrial junk—Freon canisters and chamber pots take on a life of their own. But he pulls the whole community into the fun. When locals complained that Ishtar and Ogbid looked lonely standing out there, he threw a wedding complete with preacher, cake, reception, and bird seed to throw (instead of rice) there at the corner, then carted the 1,400-pound wedding couple off for their honeymoon. A couple of weeks later they returned with Nimrod. (Gestation period of robots is sort of undetermined at this time.) It wasn't long (how long is a mystery) until little Offazzie joined the family, and a cute little thing she is, too. Cousin It was then joined by "The Reaper," and the happy family spent its days watching the road. But this is the real world, and there are bad people in it. One dark and stormy night, little Nimrod was kidnapped. J.C. and his wife offered a reward for his return, but to no avail. Then a neighbor called. He had found Nimrod in a field beaten to a fare-thee-well. J.C. took the pickup out there and brought him home. He was in intensive care for a long time as J.C. worked to bring him back to life. Since the street isn't safe anymore, Carter brought little Offazzie and the cousins home, leaving Ishtar and Ogbid lonely sentinels by the road, their sheer weight making them safe from kidnappers. Now **Carter's Gallery** has opened so all of J.C's creations can be displayed, just up the road from where the two stand. Call Carter at (816) 747–5506 to see these wonderful creatures. Bring a camera, it would make Carter and his "family" very happy.

Bristle Ridge Winery, between Warrensburg and Knob Noster, is ½ mile south of Highway 50 at Montserrat and produces quality wines that range from subtle dry whites to bright sweet reds. It sits on a hill with a panoramic view, the perfect spot to picnic with a bottle of wine, bread, cheese, and summer sausage—all sold at Bristle Ridge. Open Saturdays 10:00 A.M. to 5:00 P.M. and Sunday noon until 5:00 P.M. Closed January, February, and holidays (816–229–0961).

Look up while driving through Knob Noster, because there are interesting things in the air above Whiteman Air Force Base. The previously very, very, top secret Stealth Bomber calls this base home, and its eerie Batman-like silhouette can be seen low in the sky on approach to the base's runway. If you see it, you might as well pull off to the side of the road—as everyone else is doing—to watch it land.

THE OZARKS

Cole Camp is a tiny town that would be easy to miss, but don't. The first place to stop, if you have planned this right and it is lunchtime, is ❖ **Der Essen Platz** (816–668–3080). It's on the corner—you can't miss it, the town is small—and it's open seven days a week. Owners Larry and Ronda Shackelford's German-style restaurant features imported beers and food and a Friday buffet from 5:00 P.M. to 9:00 P.M., April through December. Cream pies of a variety not found elsewhere (unless you come from a German neighborhood) are a specialty; try German chocolate pie with coconut, or lemon pie with sour cream, crumb topping, and whipped cream. Joyce Schlesselmann, dining room manager, brought out samples of the wurst sandwiches (a pun—laugh, don't groan!) they offer. The menu includes *kasseler rippchen* (smoked boneless pork chops served on sauerkraut), *sauerbraten* (marinated beef on a bed of spätzle and gingersnap gravy), and if you are a schnitzel fan, *schweines-chnitzel, wiener schnitzel,* and *jaeger schnitzel.*

Now waddle out of "the eating place" and turn right to **Melville's Antiques and Restoration,** 108 South Maple (816–826–6570). Owner Rory Melville will take you on a tour of his sawdust-covered workshop, where he specializes in the restoration of antiques. Detail work includes brass and copper polishing, chair caning, and veneer repair. Melville also has three buildings full of antiques that look as they did when great-grandmother first bought them. Specializing in top quality golden oak and Victorian walnut furniture, he also has a large assortment of turn-of-the-century brass lighting fixtures and offers expert antique lamp restoration.

Pick up a copy of the *Antiques and Shop Guide* and stroll around town. You will find many, many places to poke around.

While you are in Cole Camp, stop by **Jim Maxwell's shop,** 113 Main Street, right around the corner from Der Essen Platz, and take a look at his caricature woodcarvings. The finely detailed carvings feature Missouri coal miners, gangsters, artillery men from the Civil War, and doughboys of World War I. The limited edition carvings are original pieces of art sought after by collectors. Maxwell is the author of two woodcarving books and creates a variety of subjects from casually styled Ozark Hill people to very accurately detailed caricatures of other bygone eras. Call (816) 668-2466 for more information.

About 3 miles east of Cole Camp on Highway 52 is a pretty little shop sitting alone by the side of the road. It's **Calico Country Cupboard** (816–668–4896), where owner Sally Howell features handmade country clocks, quilts and gifts. Hours are 10:00 A.M. to 5:00 P.M. daily, and Sunday noon to 6:00 P.M. (closed Tuesday). Winter hours vary.

Take a left (north) on Highway 152 between Cole Camp and Stover and drive to Highway M. Right at the intersection you will find **Orland Pennel's Craft Shop.** Orland will custom make any kind of swing, lounge chair, birdhouse, or glider in his wood-work shop there in the shed by his house. He also has some items all ready to load up and take away stacked in a gazebo in the yard. Call (314) 377–4770 to be sure he is home; he doesn't keep any regular hours, and that's just the way he wants it.

Highway 52 runs into Highway 5 at the city of Versailles (pronounced just as it looks, not the French way). Versailles is the gateway to the Lake of the Ozarks area. Here you make the decision to go east on Highway 52 to the St. Louis side of the lake or southwest on Highway 5 to the Kansas City side. But before you decide anything, drive to the square and check out **Omi's Apple Haus,** 100 North Fisher (314–378–5491). It opened in the fall of 1989. Omi's (German for "grandma") sells handmade items from local Mennonites: quilts, mincemeat, honey, dolls, and dresses and bonnets for little girls. From Monday through Saturday from 9:00 A.M. until 4:00 P.M. you can eat German bratwurst or have one of its famous baked apple dumplings. At Omi's you can pick up a brochure listing the other shops in town.

Just a half block southeast of the square at 206 Jasper, a brick walkway leads to a two-story white Victorian home that has now become the **Hilty Inn Bed and Breakfast.** This elegant home built in 1877 has four rooms with private baths. Owner Doris Hilty knows her way around the area and can guide you in your shopping or lake fun. If a quiet afternoon is what you want, though, there is a sitting room and a gift shop in which to browse. Doris carries books by local writers (this book can be purchased there) and crafts by area Mennonites. The East bedroom has a private front porch, and there is a screened side porch with swings for the other guests. A good breakfast with gourmet coffee and tea is part of the package. Call (314) 378–2020 for more information.

The Lake of the Ozarks area is called the "Land of the Magic Dragon." If you look at the lake on a map and go snake-eyed, it has a dragon shape; hence the name. The Ozark heritage stems from the first immigrants here who were from Tennessee, Kentucky, and nearby parts of the southern Appalachians. The Upper-South hill-country folks were descended from Scottish-Irish stock.

For many years the Ozark Mountains sheltered these folks and few outsiders entered the area; you may have heard of the Irish Wilderness. Because of the rough topography, the railroads avoided the area, and this extreme isolation until about fifty years ago created the "Ozark Hillbilly." The values, lifestyle, and beliefs of those first settlers are still much in evidence.

The building of Bagnell Dam to form the Lake of the Ozarks eroded that isolation and turned the area into the Midwest's summer playground. Because it is not a Corps of Engineers lake, homes can be built right on the water's edge; the 1300 miles of serpentine shore is more shoreline than the state of California has!

Miles of lake coves, wooded hills, and steep dusty roads are still unsettled. Most undeveloped areas have no roads at all leading to them. The east side of the lake, which houses the dam, has become the drop-in tourist side. The track is beaten slick over here. There are restaurants, shopping malls, and water slides galore.

Some of the unique places on the east side deserve a mention before you head to the west side of the lake, where the more fascinating spots hide. If you go to Bagnell Dam from Eldon, watch for wintering eagles—here and at most of the lake crossings. They retreat from the Arctic chill up north, following flocks of migrating geese.

You may not have thought of Missouri as a big state for bald eagle watching—and spring through early fall, it's not, though a captive breeding program of the Missouri Department of Conservation has been in effect since 1981 to reestablish a wild breeding population. But come winter, these big birds take up residence wherever they can find open water and plentiful feeding. One recent year, over 1400 bald eagles were counted, making this state second only to Washington in the lower forty-eight states for eagle sightings. At most Missouri lakes, their main diet consists of fish—they have far better luck with fishing than most humans.

Taking the back way around the lake along Highway 52 to Eldon and then Highway 54 to Bagnell Dam is more interesting than the much-traveled and very crowded Highway 5/54 route.

A left turn (north) on Highway 5 puts you in the middle of the Mennonite community. On the roads around Versailles, horse-drawn buggies carry Mennonite citizens on their daily tasks. They are less strict than the Jamesport Amish—the somber black attire is uncommon—and most of the homes have telephones and electricity, though many don't. Old Order Mennonite women wear prayer bonnets but dress in printed fabrics. Some families have cars, but many of the cars are painted black—chrome and all. To get a good tour of the area, begin on Highway 5 at Versailles and follow it to a sign announcing the turnoff for Lehmans' if you plan to be in the area a couple of days.

❖ **Lehmans'** (816–337–6272) is a couple of miles off Highway 5 on Route 2 (watch for the sign). This is a not-so-well-kept secret and popular with the locals, but tourists are unaware of it, for the most part. Mennonites Carl and Anna Mary Lehman and their daughter Barbara welcome you to this private home about 1½ miles off Highway 5. Another daughter, Ginny, serves guests and makes the fine quilts for sale here.

There are fresh vegetables in season, this morning's eggs from the barn, and homemade jam and frozen vegetables in winter. Bring wine or beer if you want to, but no hard liquor. They serve two kinds of pie with the meal, and when the season is right, fresh strawberry and peach pie or cobbler. Choose the meat when making a reservation—smoked turkey, ham, beef, or chicken—and they do the rest. The three-course dinner includes six salads, two veggies, homemade rolls, and dessert, and takes about one and a half hours; don't be in a hurry. They can seat as few as six or as many as forty using several rooms in the house. You must call twelve to twenty-four hours in advance.

Backtrack a little to where Highway 5 splits into Highway 52 and follow Highway 52 east to Highway C on the left. Stay on Highway C about 4 miles east of Highway 52 and, in the summertime, watch for **Zimmerman's Market** on the left. The Zimmermans are a Mennonite family who have a garden that covers acres of land and is worked by hand by the family. The little shop there has fresh produce to match the season, and it carries fresh milk, butter, and homemade breads, along with cheeses from other Mennonite farms in the area. Homemade noodles, sorghum molasses, honey, jelly, and fresh eggs also fill the little shop. You can call (314) 378–4836 to see what's available today.

Follow Highway C about 6 miles to ◆ **Pleasant Valley Quilts and Tea Room**. There is a sign by the road where you can turn and drive about three quarters of a mile on gravel. The Brubaker family gathers a fine selection of quilts and crafts from Mennonite families in the area. Their daughters Lydia and Lucille handle the quilt shop, where quilts of all sizes and colors are hung for display. In fact, quilts will be made to order for you if you have a particular color or style in mind. Quilts made by local Mennonite ladies join aprons, dolls, and other hand-crafted items for sale here. Daughter Marian has the tea shop, where daily special sandwiches are written on the chalkboard by the door. Call (314) 378–6151. They are open from 8:00 A.M. to 5:00 P.M. every day but Sunday.

Follow the sign off Highway C down a gravel road to the

Dutch Country Store, which carries bulk foods but also has a huge selection of freight-damaged groceries and toiletries. There are usually buggies parked out front along with the automobiles. The store always has a good selection of name-brand cereals and canned goods, shampoo and dog food, just about anything. The selection is different every week.

Turn north on Highway E, then follow E to Highway K (this sounds harder than it really is), but watch closely for horse-drawn buggies and bicycles on these hilly back roads. Highway K leads east to the tiny, tiny town of Excelsior and **Weavers' Market,** serving this community of about 250 Mennonite families. Weavers' carries fresh-frozen farm produce, frozen home-made pies ready to pop into your oven, an enormous assortment of teas and spices, and other bulk foods, including homemade noodles. Nearby (follow the signs) is **Excelsior Fabric,** where Anna and Sam Shirk and their family carry an extensive collection of quilting fabrics.

If you turn left back at Highway E on a Sunday morning about 10:00 A.M., you will come to the Clearview Mennonite Church and see dozens of horse-drawn buggies tied up in stables and at hitching posts around the church. It's quite a sight.

Also on Highway E between that church and the Bethel Mennonite Church, the Martin family offers fine home-cooked meals. Look sharp for the house, for there is only a martin house in the front yard (with a sign on it saying **Martin House**) and no other signs. Pull around to the back entrance; the restaurant is on the lower level. Anna and Harvey Martin turn out Pennsylvania Dutch meals, and you select the menu from meat through dessert. Choose from roast beef, chicken, ham, and pork ribs. There is also ham or beef meat loafs. The vegetable and salad come from the Martin garden (the fruit salad is full of fresh apples and covered with an orange sauce), the rolls are, of course, homemade, and the pies are whatever kind of fruit or cream pie you choose. This meal is only $8.00 a person, with a six-person minimum. One dollar extra gets you a second meat, $2.00 a third.) You must call twenty-four hours in advance to reserve a table, and the Martins can seat slightly more than fifty people. You may bring a bottle of wine to enjoy with your meal, if you wish. Call (314) 378–4578 for reservations.

Now find your way back to Highway 52 and take a left (east) to

Leah Zimmerman's bake shop (a sign on the highway says FARMER'S MARKET. Leah's is the first house on the left; a large sign in her yard says ❖ **Shady Oak Market.** Her buggy is near the barn, where her horse Jessica waits for excursions to the grocery store, Weavers' Market, or church on Sunday. Leah has produce from her own wonderful garden, but she also is the source for eggs from free-range chickens, fresh fruit from family orchards, and a whole range of baked goods she turns out daily. Cinnamon bread, pies with whatever fresh fruit is in season, cookies, jams, and canned goods deck her shelves in the pantry just off the front porch. The sign says COME IN and that's just what it means. She's usually in the kitchen baking something tasty—she does custom baking for regulars—and comes out when she hears the door slam. Call (314) 378-6401 to order something special (in the fall her apple dumplings are wonderful!).

The difference between the east and west sides of the lake has been described as like "flipping channels between 'Hee Haw' and 'Lifestyles of the Rich and Famous'." Welcome to the St. Louis side, a road more traveled but still lots of fun.

Highway 54 through Osage Beach is, in a word, touristy. The path here is not only beaten, it's three lanes wide and heavy with traffic in the summer—the bumper-to-bumper gridlock type you came here to get away from. The road is filled to overflowing with craft shops, flea markets, bumper cars, and water slides. There are plenty of good eating places, from fast-food chains to little places like **Wickerleigh's Porch,** where you can find a good-for-your-heart breakfast as early as 7:00 A.M. (and you can also find eggs benedict), and the **Peace-'n'-Plenty Country Cafe** in Poverty Flats Village (near State Road KK), specializing in homemade soups, sandwiches, breads, and salads.

Joe Orr is a Missouri artist who is gaining a well-deserved reputation. You can see why for yourself at his elegant new gallery/studio/home right next to TanTara on Highway KK in Osage Beach. The ❖ **Orr Gallery and Studio** also features Rita Orr's wonderful silkscreens and monoprints. But that's not all that is tucked away in this second-floor hideaway. Displayed here are Ron Schroeder's sculptures, Paul Clervi's bronze sculptures, Steve Johnson's contemporary free-form pottery, and Rhonda Cearlock's raku pottery. Joe is the founder of the National Oil and Acrylic Painters Society, which has a national

CATHY JOHNSON

Shady Oak Market

exhibition here in November with over 600 artists from thirty states entered for exhibit. Joe's and Rita's studios are on the gallery level of their home, too, and open if you want to watch them at work. Hours are from 10:00 A.M. until 5:00 P.M. daily, but Joe is quick to add that it's "sort of by chance or appointment, too," so calling ahead (314–348–2232) might be a good idea.

The **Potted Steer Restaurant** (314–348–5053) is in a comfortable-looking wooden building tucked in at the west end of the Grand Glaize Bridge on Highway 54 in Osage Beach. Owner Joseph Boer, a native of Holland who came to this country on refugee status on Christmas Day in 1956, opened the restaurant in 1971. It is a very laid-back place where casual clothes are the rule and long waits are expected. But the crowd is vacation-loose and fun. The specialty here is deep-fried lobster tail (which sounds like heresy to a seafood lover). Boer says he has never tasted the creation that made the restaurant famous. You see, he hates seafood. To tide you over until dinner arrives, order the massive onion rings. Boer also has one of the finest wine lists in the state. The restaurant is closed from the middle of November until the third Friday in March.

If you have taken the route along the west side of the lake, you will begin to see the real Ozarks now. Missouri has surprisingly diverse wildlife, from the blind cave fish to the black bear, which still forages in the heavy woods. The pileated woodpecker (the size of a chicken, no kidding!) will certainly wake you up in the morning if he decides to peck on your shake shingles. The west side of the lake is still undiscovered except by Kansas City people, who have tried to keep it quiet. Here, great eating places abound and small shops hide off the beaten path.

Highway 5 cuts like a razor slash through the hills between Gravois Mills and Laurie. There are some quiet, low-key places not to be missed.

◆ **Spring Lake Lodge and Antiques** (314–372–2201), owned by James Marci and Gordon Stallings, is no flea market. Open March to October, the shop contains fine antiques, art objects, jewelry, and decorative accessories that are as nice as those at big-city shops but priced more reasonably. The shop is closed in the winter so that the two men can travel around the country finding and buying the elegant pieces they show there. People who know about the place try to be the first ones there in the spring when the shop opens. Large walnut sideboards, Victorian sofas, and unique lamps are part of the hundreds of items in the two floors of showroom.

The bright yellow place with the two huge, hairy gorillas standing out front is the **Gorilla Burger**, and although the Gorillaburger is good, the turkey fries (don't ask) are a seasonal treat not to be passed up.

As you continue along Highway 5 through the town of Gravois Mills, you will notice a large sign pointing to **Troutdale Ranch.** It is not the spot for experienced trout fishers, but it is the perfect spot to teach the children how to cast a line (guaranteed catch) and it is the perfect place to pick up some sweet, pink-fleshed trout for dinner. There has been a trout farm here since 1932. Current owner Dorothy Gates and her son Lorin haven't changed things much. Someone will simply go out the door and net you some of the freshest trout you will ever taste. They will clean and bone it for you and pack it in ice, too. The water here is fifty-six degrees, colder than most trout waters, so the trout grow more slowly and that means better. They are farm fed, making them safe and some of the best you will ever eat. Many of the best restaurants in the metropolitan areas serve trout from the ranch. Try the smoked trout that is also for sale at the ranch. It is excellent. In fact, it's on the menu at the Blue Heron—served cold—and is a popular summer dish. Troutdale is open year-round from 7:30 A.M. until 4:30 P.M. (from November until March 1, they are closed on Sunday). Call (314) 372–6100 for information.

After Gravois Mills, you will come to the tiny **Ozark Hills Senior Citizens Craft Shop.** The store carries lovingly handcrafted crochets, knits, and pieces of needlework made by the local seniors. Also sold here are hand-carved items and almost any other kind of craft you can imagine.

Just outside of Laurie on Highway 5 is St. Patrick's Catholic Church. Father Fred Barnett is the pastor here. This unique church sits on acres of outdoor gardens that feature waterfalls, fountains, and a shrine dedicated to mothers, ✙ **The Shrine of Mary Mother of the Church.** You may add your mother's name to the list to be remembered in ongoing prayers. On summer Sundays, Mass is at 8:30 A.M. at the shrine, and casual dress is in the spirit of a Lake of the Ozarks vacation. The outdoor candlelight procession and Mass on Saturday nights at 8:30 P.M. at the shrine are beautiful and open to anyone. Times change in winter, so call Father Barnett (314-374-7855) for a current schedule.

In the town of Laurie you can turn right on Highway 135, which wanders back to Stover and Highway 52, over some genuine roller-coaster dips and beautiful unpopulated Ozark country. The next highway is State Road T. Turn left here and go 7½ miles to be exact, to find a surprise. The **Buffalo Creek Winery** sits among acres of vineyards back in the Ozark hills. Right now owner Jim Stephens' little tasting room is set among acres of grapevines. He is moving the tasting room to a spot on Buffalo Cove at the 70 mile marker so boat traffic can stop and try his interesting wines. The Concord Grape wine is light and not too sweet (not the familiar Mogen David flavor). Probably the most interesting taste is from the persimmon wine, a sweet and fruity wine made from persimmons grown on his place. Call Jim at (314) 377–4535 to find out if the new lake site is open yet.

Near the town of Greenview on Highway 5 stands a hand-hewn oak log building. Known as the ◆**Old Trail House** (314–873–5824), it overlooks the lake at the spot where one of the wagon trails going from Old Linn Creek to Arnholdt's Mill on the Big Niangua River ran across the ridge. Wagons drawn by oxen and horses forded the river at the mill. The spot is said to be an old Indian lookout point, and you can see for about 20 miles to the west from the deck, where dinner is served in good weather. A beautiful, antique oak mantel surrounds a log fire in winter. It is a favorite spot of locals. Hours are from 5:00 to 10:00 P.M. Monday through Saturday.

If you are looking for a bed and breakfast instead of a resort on the Lake of the Ozarks, check with Kay Cameron at Ozark Mountain Country Bed and Breakfast Service at (800) 695–1546 or (417) 334–4720. Kay has listings for cottages on the water in Camdenton, Osage Beach, Sunrise Beach, and other small towns around the lake.

Either way you circle the lake, east or west, you will end up in Camdenton at the intersection of highways 5 and 54. Continue west on Highway 54 and turn on Highway D to ◆**Ha Ha Tonka State Park.** High on a bluff overlooking an arm of the Lake of the Ozarks, poised over a cold, aqua blue spring that bubbles out from under a limestone bluff, are the ruins of a stone "castle" with a story to tell. There is a European feel to the ruins; it's as if you have stumbled on a Scottish stronghold here in the Missouri woods. The place was conceived in 1900 as a sixty-room retreat for prominent Kansas City businessman Robert Snyder. But tragedy struck; Snyder was killed in an automobile accident in 1906 and construction halted. Later, the castle-like mansion was completed by Snyder's son, but in 1942 a fire set by a spark from one of the many stone fireplaces gutted the buildings. All that was left were the ghostly stone walls thrust up against the sky. Ha Ha Tonka is now a state park, although the mansion is still a ghostly ruins half hidden in the trees.

The park is a classic example of karst topography, with caves and sinkholes, springs, natural bridges, and underground streams. (This typical southern Missouri geology is responsible for the many caves in the state.) There are nine nature trails here; explore on your own or check in with the park office (314–751–2479) for a naturalist-guided tour; programs are available all year long.

Ha Ha Tonka State Park

About halfway between Warsaw and Clinton on Highway 7 is the town of Tightwad (population 56) and the **Tightwad Tavern and B-B-Q** (816–477–3389). Owner Wayne Grigsby came to Tightwad in 1946 at the tender age of four. Now he chops wood and smokes meat. Hours are from 11:00 A.M. to 9:00 P.M. every day but Monday. The lounge has live music—country and good old-fashioned rock and roll—from 9:00 P.M. until 1:00 A.M., so you can get down and boogie, too. In January and February he takes it easy and just opens Friday through Sunday.

The city of Clinton is every chamber of commerce's dream come true. It has one of the most active squares in the country, filled with over 150 shops and services, and there is lots of parking. You can't miss the wonderful old courthouse and outdoor pavilion in the center of the square. The town has changed little since 1836, when it began as an outpost in the heart of the Golden Valley.

History buffs will find plenty of research material at the ◆ **Henry County Museum** at 203 West Franklin Street, just off the northwest corner of the square. The building itself was owned by Anheuser-Busch from 1886 until Prohibition. Huge blocks of ice (often cut from the nearby lake) were used to chill the kegs in the cooling room. The second room contains a skylight and double doors leading to the old loading dock and courtyard. Quick dashes in horse-drawn wagons were necessary to transport the beer while still cool to the depot where there was access to three railroads. The building houses the Courtenay Thomas room, commemorating the Clinton native who became an international operatic soprano.

Find Commercial Street in Harrisonville and hit the antiques jackpot. There are too many antiques and flea markets to mention, but it looks like three cherries on the antiques slot machine for flea-market gamblers.

CHEESE COUNTRY

Nevada (pronounced *Na-VAY-da*), south of Harrisonville on Highway 71, has a typical town square with the **Nevada Deli** (417–667–3850) on the east side. Just like New York, the deli offers real deli delights—pastrami, corned beef, dark rye, and even New York seltzer water—that are hard to find in the Midwest. Hours are 7:00 A.M. to 6:00 P.M. weekdays.

114

Here you can go west on Highway 54 to El Dorado Springs (*Da-RAY-do,* this being a very non-Spanish speaking part of the country) as a shortcut to the Osceola area.

Large dairy barns and silos built around the turn of the century are still in use, and dairy cattle—Holsteins and Guernseys—join beef cattle along the roadside. Surprise! Missouri is the third-largest cheese-producing state in the nation.

El Dorado Springs, just east of Nevada off Highway 54, is a pretty little town complete with a nostalgic bandstand in the tree-shaded park at the center of town. It looks like something straight out of *The Music Man.* There's a band here every Friday and Saturday night and Sunday afternoon; a local band has played in the park for over a hundred years. The old spa town was crowded with bathhouses and hotels, but the spa business ended long ago for most towns like this one. El Dorado Springs has done a great job of preserving itself anyway.

While in El Dorado, you can see the free museum above ✦ **Carl's Gun Shop.** Owner Carl McCallister and his son, Terry, have more than 1,000 guns in glass showcases and a fine collection of trophy-size taxidermied animal mounts, including two full-body bears, in a gymnasium-sized room. The gun shop takes up half a city block and has one of the most complete private collections of firearms in the state. You won't find any assault rifles for sale here, and there's no survivalist gear on display. The well-lighted display rooms have a staff of people who knows guns. Carl even has toy guns for sale for customers' children. The family environment makes women and children feel comfortable. Carl's wife, Terri, also works at the store. Carl's is open seven days a week from 9:00 A.M. to 6:00 P.M. Monday through Saturday, and from 9:00 A.M. to 5:00 P.M. on Sunday. It is closed from January to September. Call (417) 876-4168 for more information.

If you don't take the shortcut, you will continue down Interstate 71 to Lamar; history fans will find ✦ **Harry S Truman's Birthplace** here. (No, there is no period after the S, because the president didn't have a middle name—his folks just put an S in there.) It's a long way from this little house to the big white one on Pennsylvania Avenue in our nation's capital.

Bicyclists know a place called **Cooky's** at 825 Main in Golden City at the junction of Highway 126 and 37 south and east of

Lamar. Out of season, it's a small-town cafe on the south side of the main drag. During bike-riding season, though, Cooky's is the place to dream about when you are 300 miles out on the trail. Bikecentennial, Inc., of Missoula, Montana, put Cooky's on the map—the Transamerica Trail map, that is—and riders have flocked here ever since for some serious carbohydrate loading. It's not uncommon to watch a rider from Australia chow down on three or four pieces of Jim and Carol Elred's terrific pies; you can be more moderate, if you like. A steak dinner costs only $8.75; the home-raised beef will keep you going down the trail whether you come by car or bike. Hours are 6:00 A.M. until 8:00 P.M. Saturday through Thursday. Call (417) 537-4741 for information.

Jerry Overton, president of the Missouri Prairie Foundation, puts in a good word for ✦ **Golden Prairie,** designated a National Natural Landmark by the Federal Department of the Interior. It's not reclaimed prairie or replanted prairie—this is a virgin remnant of the thousands of acres of grassland that once covered the Midwest, important not only for the historic plants it contains, but also for the varieties of wildlife that inhabit it. Here, you can still hear the sound of the prairie chicken. Listen for them exactly 3 miles west of Golden City on Highway 126 and exactly 2 miles south of Highway 26 on the first gravel road.

If prairie chickens interest you, Karlos and Elaine Kaelke will offer you a real treat at the **Kaelke Prairie Chicken Bed & Breakfast** in Lockwood at the junction of highways 126 and 97. No, they don't fry prairie chicken for dinner, rather they celebrate the beauty of these endangered birds. Every spring the Kaelke's 1,000-acre farm becomes the "booming ground" of the local prairie chicken population. At dawn guests can watch the colorful mating dance of a dozen male chickens as they strut, dance and inflate their bright-orange air sacs to make the booming sound. The two-story brown brick farmhouse has witnessed this display every spring since the 1950s. April is the only time this farm home is open for guests, so call (417) 232-4925 early to reserve one of the four homey guest rooms. The rooms share two baths. A big farm breakfast follows the show. The price is $60 and be sure to bring your best binoculars for a really close-up view of this annual rite.

The **Bush Hotel** (antiques, bed and breakfast) in Jerico Springs north on Highway 97 is owned by Rodney and Renee

Shipley (417–398–2343 or 398–2519 when the shop is closed). The B&B was a run-down disaster when the Shipleys found it. A relic of the mineral spas popular about 1906, it was the last survivor of the many hotels in town. Now it contains eight refurbished rooms with four bathrooms to share. A different country breakfast is served each morning—perhaps biscuits-and-gravy or waffles. Rooms are $40 for one night, $35 each additional night. The weekend nearest June 9 is busy every year because of the annual Jerico Springs picnic/reunion, but for the most part the hotel caters to folks headed for Stockton Lake, because Highway B is the quickest route to the lake from Interstate 71. The shop is open Thursday through Saturday from 9:00 A.M. to 5:00 P.M.

A roadside park just outside Osceola on Highway 82 West will show you what attracted Indians and settlers to the area: the breathtaking view of the white bluffs where the Sac and Osage rivers meet. Highway 82 also has a Sac River access point and boat ramp if you are hauling a boat to the Truman reservoir.

Highway 13 bypasses the town square but is home to **◆ Osceola Cheese Shop** and **Ewe's in the Country** (417–646–8131). Mike and Marcia Bloom own both shops, which share the building. The Blooms buy the cheese in bulk and smoke and flavor it in the former cheese factory; they have been at this same location for over forty-five years. They now offer over sixty-nine varieties of cheese, mostly from Missouri, with each type cut for sampling. Try jalapeño (extra hot), instant pizza, or chocolate (yes!) cheese. Pick up a catalog; they ship cheese anywhere in the world—except from April to September, when it might arrive as hot cheese sauce. Hours are 7:30 A.M. to 7:00 P.M. weekdays at the cheese shop, 9:00 A.M. to 5:00 P.M. at the gift shop.

Take a right at the sign on Highway 13 and wander into Osceola. On the northeast corner of the town square is **Dempsey's Coach Stop.** There are many stories to be told here, if the walls could talk. With the help of artist M. E. Norton, they do. Harry Truman ate here, Jesse James slept here, and Dr. Ruth Seevers practiced here until she was ninety and had delivered more babies than anyone in the state. She died at 102, no doubt of exhaustion. The Butterfield Stage Line stopped here, and the Corps of Engineers built the Truman Dam nearby. Owners Ken and Donna Dempsey will explain each section of the montage if you are interested: the Seminole chief who never surrendered (Chief Osceola), or the time the town was burned to the ground by Jim Lane, just after the Civil War—it's wall-to-wall history. Call (417) 646-8988 for more information.

On the southwest corner of the square is the 109-year-old Commercial Hotel, now being renovated and opened as a craft shop. ❖ **Colby's Cafe,** at 107 Chestnut on the north side of the square (also in a renovated building) is where Curtis and Kathy Colby serve from-scratch meals from 6:00 A.M. to 2:00 P.M. seven days a week. Kathy is from Kansas City and says that moving to Osceola took some adjusting. "But my five kids have seen bald eagles and deer they would only have seen in the zoo," she says. The pan-fried chicken on Wednesday and Sunday ($3.85) draws a crowd. Call (417) 646-2620 for more information.

Nearby in the Old Commercial Hotel, there is a neat little pre-owned-clothing store and a surprise in the form of an espresso bar and gift shop. Owner Lynette Bullock invites you to drop in after lunch. Call (417) 464-8602 for more information.

Attics always have a trunk or two hidden away. Why not? They are fine for storing the other things we hate to throw away. When families moved here from the east, they brought their belongings in trunks and would use them as dressers, chairs, tables until real furniture would be built. Chuck Burton and Elsa Hickethier have taken it upon themselves to restore trunks to their original splendor at ❖ **The Trunk Shop** just south of Lowry City on Highway 13. Today Chuck stocks more than 100,000 trunk parts and not only restores trunks but builds them from scratch. The showroom has many antiques on sale including some in like-new condition. He can pick locks and get your trunk open and then make a key for it, too. Call (417) 644-2846. The Trunk Shop is open from 8:00 A.M. until 5:00 P.M. every day but Saturday when the shop closes at 4:30 P.M.

NORTHWEST MISSOURI

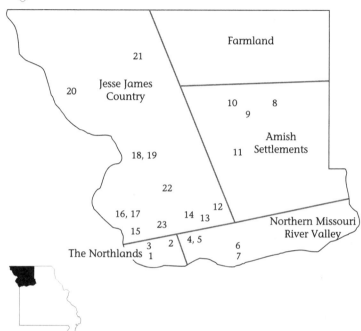

Farmland

21

Jesse James
Country

20

10   8
9

Amish
Settlements

18, 19   11

22

16, 17   14 13   12
15   23

The Northlands 3 2 4, 5   6
1   7

Northern Missouri
River Valley

1. Acapulco
2. Nichols Pottery Shop
   and Studio
3. Hodge Park
4. Corbin Mill Place
5. Martha Lafite Thompson
   Nature Sanctuary
6. Ray County Museum
7. G.G.'s Country Pantry
   and Fudge Factory
8. Jamesport
9. McDonald's Tea Room
10. Adam-Ondi-Ahman Shrine
11. J.C. Penney Memorial Library
    and Museum
12. Elms Hotel

13. Watkins Woolen Mill
    State Historic Site
14. Jesse James Farm Historic Site
15. English Landing
16. McCormick Distilling
    Company
17. The Vineyards
18. Albrecht Art Museum
19. St. Joseph Hospital
    Psychiatric Museum
20. Squaw Creek National
    Wildlife Refuge
21. Conception Abbey
22. Candyman's Mule Barn
23. Smithville Lake

Northwest Missouri

It gets cold in northwest Missouri—make no mistake—especially near the northernmost border, where the plains are chilled by every stiff wind howling down from the frigid north. Alberta Clipper, Siberian Express, whatever you call it, Missouri catches hell in the winter, bringing to mind that old joke: "There's nothing between here and the North Pole but two bobwire (barbed wire) fences, and one o' them's down." In 1989 all records were broken—along with that fence—when the nighttime temperature bottomed out at minus twenty-three degrees (wind chill made that sixty degrees below zero). It also gets hot in Missouri; August days can soar over the one hundred-degree mark.

But at its temperate best, Jesse James Country is a great place to visit that's filled with great hideouts. (James knew them all. It seems that, like George Washington, Jesse James slept almost everywhere—in northwest Missouri anyway.)

Not that that's all there is to this section of the state; we'd hate to say we're living in the past on the rather unsavory reputation of our own "Robbing" Hood. There is a national wildlife refuge on the central flyway that is absolutely essential to migrating waterfowl. There is Excelsior Springs, where folks once came to take the waters and where Harry S Truman heard he had lost the presidential election to Thomas Dewey—at least according to the *Chicago Tribune*.

The Northlands

North Kansas City is just across the Missouri River from the town with a similar name. This is a separate city, with a healthy industrial tax base and a coordinated downtown shopping area complete with plazas, fountains, and wide streets. "Northtown" has its own mayor, its own police department, and its own quirky charm. There are cafes and delis and bakeries; North Kansas Citians know how to eat.

About 42 years ago, Rafael Jimenez and his wife Socorro opened a little restaurant in Kansas City serving the Mexican food they knew so well. He never advertised but day after day, the place was full of people. They came for lunch, they came for dinner, they came on a whim, because they were craving something. And business was good at the ◆**Acapulco.** The Jimenezes turned out dishes based on old family recipes, and people filled the little restaurant every day and stood in line on weekends. Today the new and larger Acapulco Restaurant is in North Kansas City at 1041 Burlington Avenue. Rafael is more or less retired (he still shows up often) and his son Gustavo now owns the restaurant. Gus is more modern. He is thinking seriously about doing some advertising. The best advertising he does, though, is word of mouth. Once your mouth gets around the food he serves—Mexican chili made with big chunks of pork served with thick, soft, corn tortillas; tamales with rich masa surrounding shredded pork; and paper thin tortilla chips with fresh salsa—you tell friends about it. And the secret, somehow, gets out. For more information call (816) 472–8689.

Tiny Avondale is slightly off Highway 210 as you leave North Kansas City. Here you'll discover ◆**Nichols Pottery Shop and Studio** at 2615 Bell (816–452–0880). Deanna Nichols handcrafts stoneware that is both beautiful and functional. "You can hang it on a wall, or take it down and serve from it," she says. The studio is filled with examples of her work, and not only mugs and platters, but also intricate, earthy fountains some 32 inches high. She does custom work, lamps, and dinnerware. Browse through the shop Tuesday through Saturday from 10:00 A.M. to 5:00 P.M. A garden full of shrubs and trees interesting in all four seasons has been added to the side of the building.

As long as you are here, check out **Avondale Furniture and Antiques** at 2600 North Highway 10. Hours are catch-as-catch-can; call (816) 452–2690 for an appointment if you prefer. Owner Lillian Waskovsky has an auction service and warehouse and likes to move pieces quickly. This place may not be glitzy, but the prices are very right.

Hayes Hamburgers at 2502 N.E. Vivion Road (at Antioch Road) serves the kind of hamburgers that you could order before "fast food" was invented. This is the place to go for a hamburger after a football game or late at night on a date you didn't want to end. The hamburgers are small and made of fresh chopped meat rolled into a ball and mashed onto the grill with a handful of onions. The aroma of onions and hamburger grilling together sparks an appetite. People buy them by the bag and have been known to eat a dozen. The chili is all-American good, too. The diner is open all the time—twenty-four hours a day.

Take the Highway 435 exit north off Interstate 35 and keep an eye out for Highway 152. A right turn will take you to ❖ **Hodge Park,** a fine place to get away from the "two Ps": progress and people.

Those big, hairy critters you spot as you enter the park are American bison; the Kansas City Zoo maintains a small herd here, where once there were thousands. Elk and deer share the enclosure; you may be able to get "up close and personal" with some of the Midwest's largest indigenous animals.

If human history is more your thing, park your car in the lot and keep walking. Shoal Creek, Missouri (816–444–4363), is a restored frontier town at Hodge Park, full of historic buildings moved here by the Kansas City Parks and Recreation Department. The tiny, two-story jail built of monolithic limestone blocks (how did they lift those things?) came from nearby Missouri City. What a place for a lockup! Local ne'er-do-wells slept off Saturday night festivities here some one hundred years ago. Other buildings include square-hewn log cabins, a one-room schoolhouse, a barn, a replica of an old mill complete with mill wheel and race, and some pretty fine houses for the gentry. Stop by during one of their living history weekends for a re-creation of frontier life, you'll feel as if you've stepped back a century. Fine nature trails lead into the woods from Shoal Creek.

If you are interested in archaeology and the peoples that inhabited this land before Europeans moved in, get yourself to Line Creek Park at 5940 Northwest Waukomis. This is a Hopewell Culture site, where Native Americans lived and worked from approximately 50 B.C. to A.D. 200. The museum houses artifacts found on the spot and in the surrounding areas.

The Kansas City Parks and Recreation Department operates the site, and schoolchildren from grade four up come for mock "digs" (artifacts are salted back into the ground so that the kids have the excitement of discovery). Hours may vary; call (816) 444–4363. You can also take your chances; the museum is usually open Saturdays and Sundays from 11:00 A.M. to 4:00 P.M. There's no charge for the museum, but for reservations for group programs, call the above number; there is a small fee for groups.

NORTHERN MISSOURI RIVER VALLEY

Head east back on Highway 152 and you'll come to historic Liberty. The downtown square has been restored to Civil War-era glory, with authentic paint colors and fancy trim—most of it original.

On the south side of the square is the **Hardware Cafe** at 5 East Kansas (816–792–3500), the latest incarnation of the old Boggess Hardware Store. Soups and salads are hearty and delicious, and entrees are never boring; if you like tearoom-style food and plenty of it, this is the place. Dessert lovers skip the meal and go right for the goodie tray. Try the "Robert Redford." We won't tell you what's in it, but once you sink your teeth into this confection you'll never miss the real thing. Prices are reasonable; two can lunch for just over $10. Lunch hours are Monday through Saturday 11:00 A.M. to 2:00 P.M., dinner is served Tuesday through Thursday until 9:00 P.M. and Friday and Saturday until 10:00 P.M.

Off the square at 111 North Water Street is a quiet little restaurant in an old Victorian home. It is now called **Water Street Place.** Owner Tim McMillian serves fresh salmon, Iowa beef (prime rib and steaks), and good home cooking. Hours are from 11:00 A.M. to 8:00 P.M. Monday through Thursday and until 9:00 on Friday and Saturday. Lunch is served until 4:00 P.M. Call (816) 792–1144 for more information.

The restored ◆**Corbin Mill Place** (816–781–3100) is now a compendium of six specialty shops housed in an old brick mill, among them **Sandy's Antiques** and a terrific selection of fabrics and supplies (as well as classes) at the **Liberty Quilt Shoppe.** Also there are the **Coffee Mill,** with a fine assortment of fresh coffee beans, and the **Old Mill Stitchery.** Behind the mill is **Bratcher Cooperage,** where you can watch the cooper turn out kegs and churns. It is open Monday through Saturday from 10:00 A.M. until 5:30 P.M.

Under the same roof is **Corbin Mill Restaurant,** where Sandy—of the antique shop—and her daughter turn out home cooking for the lunchtime crowd in Liberty from 11:00 A.M. to 3:00 P.M. Monday through Saturday. They make a fabulous Reuben sandwich, and prices are moderate.

Sandy and Tom Williams opened the mill in 1986 as an outgrowth of their original antiques store a few blocks away, and now they offer a great place to spend an afternoon—it just keeps growing. The mill, with its 24–inch-thick limestone foundation and 18–inch brick walls, is built on an original land grant from President James Monroe for relief from the 1811 New Madrid earthquake (that event had far-reaching consequences!). Corbin Mill Place is open at 131 South Water from 10:00 A.M. to 5:00 P.M. Monday through Saturday.

There are three museums in downtown Liberty, either on the square or within easy walking distance, among them the **Jesse James Bank Museum Historic Site** and the **Mormon Jail Museum.** The town is chock-full of antiques and craft shops, so plan on browsing. You can pick up a map at Corbin Mill.

The ◆**Martha Lafite Thompson Nature Sanctuary** (816–781–8598) offers a wonderful place to watch the wildlife, take a naturalist-guided walk, or enjoy special programs—from making your own bird feeder to learning about the constellations on a night hike. Over 600 species of plants and many fish, reptiles, amphibians, and mammals make their homes here, and over 160 species of birds have been sighted. Worn out? Take in the lovely new sanctuary building with its displays of indigenous plants, or watch snapping turtles and catfish in the creek-habitat aquarium. Enjoy one of their many programs. Relax on the spacious deck in redwood Adirondack chairs, or buy a book, a bird feeder, or bird call to take home. Watch for the sanctuary sign at 407 North La Frenz Road.

Take Highway 210 through the tiny towns of Missouri City, Orrick, Fleming, and Camden, which are dotted along the Missouri River. The views are spectacular, especially from the observation stop just this side of Missouri City. At your back is Nebo Hill, an important site for prehistoric Indians who found this a perfect place for ceremonies and camps; the site was in use for hundreds of years. After a good spring rain you're liable to see artifact hunters out in the fields nearby.

As you pass through tiny Missouri City, which gamely survived the flood of '93, watch for the AAA-rated stone elementary school that has reaped national attention in *Reader's Digest* and *Newsweek;* it is one school that really works.

Highway 210 will take you to Richmond. Here the ◆**Ray County Museum** occupies a beautiful old brick home on West

Royle Street (816–776–2305). The Y-shaped building is unusual in itself, and the contents will tell you much about this area, from pre-Civil War days to the present. A special natural history section highlights indigenous wildlife.

To find the museum, go past the four-way stop at the edge of town on Highway 210 to Royle Street, and west to the large brick building atop the hill on the left. The library is open Wednesday through Sunday from noon until 4:00 P.M., but call for the new museum hours, which changed after its recent remodeling. If you are here the first weekend in October, you'll find mountain men, trappers, and traders as well as old-time arts and crafts at the Old Trails Festival on the grounds of the museum.

The Richmond area is also home to several unusual shops. Five miles north on Highway 13 is **The Farmer's Daughter Antiques** owned by Bob and Rilla Simmons (816–776–2936). Here you will find country furniture and all kinds of Americana, Monday through Friday from 11:00 A.M. to 4:00 P.M. and weekends by chance.

Just up Highway 10 between Richmond and Carrollton is a **museum of hammers** in Norborne. Yes, you heard right— hammers. Glen Albrecht has a shed full of them. This semiretired farmer with a terrific sense of humor has collected hammers of all shapes, sizes, and applications and displays them neatly hung and labeled. It's an amazing array, as visitors from all over— including Europe and Japan—will attest. Glen insists it's not really a museum, just a collection. It's a big one. Admission is free, but hours are catch-as-catch-can at 405 Elmwood. Call Glen at (816) 594–3455 to make sure he's not out on the "north forty."

The highway between Richmond and Lexington passes through the town of Henrietta and then over the old Lexington bridge. While in Henrietta, stop by ◆ **G.G.'s Country Pantry and Fudge Factory** and load up on chocolate. They are open Wednesday through Saturday from 10:00 A.M. to 5:00 P.M. **Whistle Stop Antiques** is a new shop right down the road, so you have an excuse beyond chocolate to drive to Henrietta.

AMISH SETTLEMENTS

Chillicothe is a very special small town; don't pass it by.

Remember that gorgeous blond of 1930s movies fame, Jean

Harlow? The folks in Chillicothe do, every time they dine at **Harlow's** (816–646–6812). The lady's photos adorn every wall, reminding us what glamour was all about. It's tablecloth dining at 609 Jackson, but it's casual. Cliff and Kathy Harlow are proud of their blue-ribbon-winning batter-fried turkey breast. Entrees range in price from $5.95 to $18.95. Hours are 11:00 A.M. to 9:30 P.M. Monday through Friday. It's dinner only on Saturday from 4:00 until about 10:00 P.M.

North on Highway 65 is the town of Trenton. Don't mistake Trenton Cemetery Prairie for a neglected eyesore, with its rough grasses obscuring some of the old tombstones. Established in 1830, its protected status as a cemetery happily resulted in one of the few precious parcels of native prairie remaining in the state. Today it is maintained by the Missouri Conservation Department. Preservation is especially crucial; prairie north of the Missouri River is scarce. These patchwork remnants produce the seeds adapted to the northern Missouri climate that are essential to reestablishing prairie ecosystems.

This is an area of oddities; what you see may not be what you get. Riverside Country Club (816–359–6004), Trenton's golf course, has tree stumps carved into life-size animals around the fairways. (If you hit a birdie or an eagle around here, it may be a wooden one.) Former greens keeper Don McNabb was an artist with a chainsaw and has salted the nine-hole course with bears and other critters. The club is open for golf to anyone for the cost of a greens fee (and cart rental, if you wish), but nongolfers are welcome to check out the carvings.

What's it like to live like a governor? You can find out for yourself. Hosts Robert and Carolyn Brown offer lodging in former Governor Arthur Hyde's mansion at 418 East Seventh Street (816–359–5631). The 1950s **Hyde Mansion Bed and Breakfast** was completely renovated by the Browns. The large dining room contains several small tables for more intimate breakfasts. Carolyn takes individual orders for country breakfasts, unless there is a full house. Then a buffet breakfast is served from the commercial-size kitchen. There are five bedrooms; the living room and its baby grand piano are all yours. In fact, they recently added a nine-foot-long pool table. Rooms, all with private baths, are $55 to $85. Hyde's is near enough to Jamesport to fill up on festival weekends, so make your reservations early.

◆ **Jamesport** is a different world. It is the largest Mennonite settlement in Missouri and home to the most orthodox "horse and buggy" Mennonites. Here the Amish wear black, fasten clothes with pins, and allow no electricity in their homes. Don't ask the Amish to pose for pictures, though; it's against their beliefs.

The Doll House is a great B&B if you happen to love toys. The owner does, and she furnishes the place with all the goodies you remember from your childhood. She owns a doll shop in Kansas; reach her at (913) 432–2939, or call (816) 684–6333 for reservations.

There are over fifty shops in Jamesport, but only one of the Amish businesses, **Anna's Bake Shop,** is actually inside the city limits; even so, the bakery's address is Route 1. Pick up a map to the Amish shops and attractions at any of the town's businesses. **The Rolling Hills Store** offers sturdy dry goods at excellent prices (talk about natural fiber fabrics!), plus boots and shoes. **Sherwood Quilts and Crafts** has a bed piled high with handmade quilts; dig through till you find the one you can't live without. Gardeners, don't miss **Mast Greenhouse,** where you can stock your herb garden with aromatic plants that are as healthy as they come. **H & M Country Store** is a bulk-foods store with spices, herbs, and any kind of noodle you desire; the emphasis is on health and freshness. Just behind the country store, and down the hill, is a new shop called **Cookies, Books, and More.** You may have noticed that no phone numbers are included here; the Amish don't have them, making that map all the more essential.

Don't overlook the regular businesses in town, especially if you're hungry. The Mennonite-owned **Gingerich Dutch Pantry Restaurant and Bakery** (816–684–6212) can fix you a big, Amish-style meal, then take you on a tour around the area; it is open on Friday and Saturday from 6:30 A.M. until 8:00 P.M. and Tuesday through Thursday until 6:00 P.M. Early birds and night owls may want to try the **Country Cupboard,** open Tuesday to Sunday 6:00 A.M. to 9:00 P.M.

Gallatin has always been another favorite day trip for folks from the Kansas City area, mainly because of ◆**McDonald's Tea Room** (816–663–2021), known to generations of Missourians. There is just something about this place that draws a crowd—people drive miles to eat here. It could be the great home cooking, or the quiet ambience. Or it could be the strawberry shortcake done in layers of pastry and buried in whipped cream. Look for McDonald's big sign on Grand Street—this one isn't golden arches. The tearoom is open 11:00 A.M. to 3:00 P.M. Sunday through Thursday and until 8:00 P.M. on Friday and Saturday nights.

A beautiful painted-lady Victorian home is at 212 West Van Buren. It is the **Ray Home Bed and Breakfast** and is on the National Register. The carved central staircase and its six fireplaces recall an elegant time. It's worth a drive-by just to see, but if you want to spend some time there, call (800) 301–STAY.

The Mormons settled in western Daviess County in the 1830s. Just north and west of Gallatin (take Highway 13 north and turn west on Highway P) is the historic ❖ **Adam-Ondi-Ahman Shrine,** believed by Mormons to be the place where Christ will return. Northwest Missouri is important historically to the Mormon people; there were once thousands of them here. The majority were forced out during the Mormon Wars, when the state militia was ordered to drive them out of Missouri. The town of Far West, now no more than a historical marker, was comprised of 5,000 souls, all exterminated or driven from their homes. Many died during a forced march in this land of religious freedom. The marker is off Highway 13, west on Highway HH and north on Highway D, near Shoal Creek (just northwest of Kingston).

Ever wonder where retail giant J.C. Penney got his start? No, not New York, or even Chicago. It was right here in Hamilton in 1895 that he got his first job at Hale's Department Store. By the time he returned to Hamilton to buy his old employer's place of business in 1924, it was number 500 in his chain of stores. The motto of the J.C. Penney Company was "Honor, confidence, service and cooperation"—no wonder he did so well.

The ❖ **J.C. Penney Memorial Library and Museum** (816–583–9997), uptown on Davis Street, is open Tuesday through Saturday from 10:00 A.M. to 5:00 P.M. You'll love the displays of early merchandise—makes you wonder who wore the stuff. The Penney farm cottage has also been restored.

Even cattlemen like this area's history. J.C. Penney once raised great herds of Angus, and at the Penney farm there is a monument—a big monument—to Penney's prize bull.

JESSE JAMES COUNTRY

Take the Business 69 exit to Excelsior Springs. Once a magnet for people who wished to "take the waters," this old spa has enough moxie to try for a comeback. The health-spa ship was scuttled in the 1950s when an article in the *Saturday Evening Post* declared mineral waters an ineffective form of treatment; the demise was clinched when Missouri passed a bill prohibiting advertising by doctors, so now we enjoy the waters—and the baths and massages—for the lovely, hedonistic fun of it.

Visit the **Hall of Waters** at 201 East Broadway, the world's longest mineral-water bar, and sample some of the waters that attracted thousands near the turn of the century. There are more naturally occurring types of mineral waters here than anyplace else on earth except the German city of Baden-Baden, which ties Excelsior Springs.

For a truly sybaritic experience, check the schedule for baths and massage, also at the Hall of Waters (816–637–0752); Linda Hyatt operates the newly restored spa. Call (816) 630–0753 for an appointment to "take the waters," as they used to say. The steam bath (to open your pores), mineral bath (to cure what ails you), and massage (*sigh*) is $40 for one hour or $60 for ninety minutes. The lovely Art Deco-style building, built in 1937 as "the finest and most complete health resort structure in the U.S.," is a fine example of a WPA project begun during the Great Depression. Moreover, how many towns have city offices that are shared with mineral baths and massage rooms—not to mention a 25–meter indoor pool.

If you like old-fashioned burgers, don't miss **Ray's Lunch,** on Broadway. The hash browns are *killer* good. Downtown the old **Mill Inn Restaurant** looks vaguely south-of-the-border. Inside you'll find wonderful cinnamon rolls (if you can beat the local farmers to them!), peanut butter pie and, on Wednesday and Saturday only, homemade bread pudding.

What do Harry S Truman, Al Capone, and Franklin D. Roosevelt have in common? They all stayed at the ◈ **Elms Hotel** (816–630–2141) at Elms Boulevard and Regent Street. You can, too; the hotel was rescued from bankruptcy in 1979 and restored to provide a spa experience in English Tudor surroundings. Visit the environmental rooms with their saunas, hot tubs, and gentle, rainlike showers; take a steam bath and massage; stuff yourself at a sumptuous Sunday brunch in the ballroom; take a surrey ride around town; or just enjoy the beautiful grounds—artists often choose this area to hone their skills.

129

Jesse James Farm

Mineral Water Well, Excelsior Springs

Trust Falls

Octagonal Schoolhouse, Watkins Mill

Elms Hotel, Excelsior Springs

Attractions in and around Excelsior Springs

Rates are $79 for rooms, $130 for suites, and $150 for condos. The restaurant is open from 7:00 A.M. until 9:00 P.M. and until 10:00 P.M. on Friday and Saturday. Downstairs the Pump and Paddle Lounge offers late night dancing.

If it's sunday morning, you are welcome at **St. Luke's Episcopal Church** across the street. This lovely old stone church matches the Elms Hotel. Service is at 10:00 A.M. (9:00 A.M. in the summer).

Excelsior Springs also has one of the most beautiful old golf courses in the Kansas City-area and it's a municipal course, so it's affordable. Rolling hills, big trees, and surrounding woodlands make it challenging, watered fairways and paved cart paths make it pleasant year-round, and there are no bunkers, which keeps play moving smoothly (so leave your sand wedge in the car). If you go into the snack bar for a cold drink, don't miss the tiny log cabin tucked *inside* the clubhouse. It's one of the original structures in this old town, and lets you see how Missouri settlers once lived. Then at the bottom of Golf Hill Drive as you leave the area, you can stop and take a walk along the Fishing River path to see a new view of this old town—here you'll find one of the original mineral water wells towering over the park.

Viginti's Coffee House, nearby at 453 Thompson Avenue, serves flavored coffee and Italian soda. Often there are live "jam sessions" on Friday and Saturday nights. They serve good sandwiches, too.

The **Old Bank Museum,** 101 East Broadway (816–637–3712) preserves spa-town history. (Check out the dentist's office and thank your lucky stars this is the 1990s.) Look up to find a pair of murals; they're wonderful copies of Jean-François Millet's "The Gleaners" and "The Angelus," painted by an itinerant artist with more talent than fame. You can buy postcards, homemade lye soap, or a museum membership (for $1.00); you may find the Women's Auxiliary of the museum quilting or weaving rag rugs when you visit on a Wednesday. The chamber of commerce is here; Sally Dixon will fill you in on local happenings.

For a straight shot back to Kansas City, you can take Highway 69 west; but plan to stop along the way at the **Old Crockery Restaurant and Antiques** (816–635–9058) near Mosby, a mile or 3 outside of Excelsior Springs. This place sits beside glassy lakes where you can fish, walk, camp, or just sit and enjoy the geese and cormorants and herons—or whatever other opportunistic birds have found the pay fishing lakes; the birds fish free. The restaurant used to be billed as Steak and Bait, with a nod to the pay lakes; somehow this is more appetizing, though you can still get bait nearby. The food is good, country-style, and plentiful; you can buy Amish bulk goods here, as well. When you're done, browse among the antiques for a fun experience all in one place.

If you have a bit longer, turn west off Highway 69 onto Highway 92 to Watkins Mill State Park near Lawson. Follow the signs to the ❖ **Watkins Woolen Mill State Historic Site** and get ready to walk back in time. The decades fall away like leaves as you wander down the footpath from the parking area. You pass deep Missouri woods, then a tiny stone-walled cemetery where the gravestones are encrusted with lichen. Farther along the path a brick giant rises to your right, and a graceful mansion crowns the hill to your left. A young belle could make quite an entrance down the lovely, curved walnut staircase in the entryway—and probably did, more than once.

Waltus Watkins built his empire here around 1850, in the years before the Civil War. Quite an empire it was: the three-story brick mill employed dozens, providing woolen fabrics to the area. The milling machinery, from washing vats to looms, is still intact, providing pristine examples of early industrial ingenuity. The house and its outbuildings reflect a gracious life—the reward for hard work and hard-headed business sense.

Before it became a state park, the mill seemed destined for destruction. The family was selling it after more than a century of occupancy, and the place was on the auction block. Representatives from the Smithsonian were on hand to bid on rare equipment—but the day was saved, along with the integrity of the mill complex, when private individuals bought the site lock, stock, and barrel (and there were a few of those about). Eventually they were able to pass the mill complex along to the state of Missouri, and now you can tour the mill and the elegant home on the hill, participate in living history weekends (try not to miss the Victorian Christmas), or watch an ongoing archaeological dig intended to discover still more about day-to-day life one hundred years ago and more. Tours are given Monday through Saturday from 10:00 A.M. till 4:00 P.M. and Sunday from 11:00 A.M. till 4:00 P.M. Winter hours are 11:00 A.M. till 4:00 P.M.

Admission is $1.25 for adults, and 75 cents for children under twelve. Special events are usually free. A new interpretive center opened in 1992 and acts as museum and buffer between now and the nineteenth century.

A brick church and an octagonal schoolhouse are nearby, all restored to their original condition. The Watkins children and those of mill workers and local farmers attended to their readin', 'ritin', and 'rithmetic here. See the schoolhouse when it's open, if you can; call (816) 296-3357. The ventilation system of windows high in the octagonal clerestory turret is ingenious. Sunlight reflects softly around the white-painted walls inside; not much artificial light would have been necessary, with the tall windows on every side.

The park also has a 5–mile-long bike path through the woods as well as a sandy beach for swimming in the lake.

History buffs should look for the ❖**Jesse James Farm Historic Site** (816–628–6065) just off Highway 92 on Jesse James Drive, between Excelsior Springs and Kearney (watch for signs). The white house with its gingerbread trim and cedar roof sits just over a rise, a little way back from the road; the new asphalt drive and path make the place handicapped accessible. The original part of the house is a log cabin, which was recently rescued from a precarious slide into decay. The cabin contains, among other things, the remains of Jesse's original coffin, which was exhumed when the body was moved to nearby Kearney; the family originally buried him in the yard to keep the body from being disturbed by those bent on revenge or souvenirs. The coffin is odd by today's standards; there was a glass window at face level—presumably for viewing the body, not for providing a window on eternity for the deceased!

July 17, 1995, was a big day in nearby Kearney. The body buried in Jesse's grave was exhumed for DNA testing to finally settle the debate about who, exactly, was buried in the James family plot. Jesse's ancestors offered DNA samples and another man who claims that *his* grandfather is buried in Jesse's grave also offered his DNA for testing. People who believe that James died in 1950 at a very old age as well as people who believe it is Jesse's body in Mt. Olivet Cemetery brought folding chairs that morning to watch. "You goin' to the digging?" was the question asked at Clem's Cafe when it opened early that morning. By closing time, lots of people were wearing "We Dig Jesse" T-shirts that Pat Dane, the enterprising owner of **Maggie's Attic** across the street from the cemetery at the intersection of highways 92 and 33 had sold to all the network cameramen and reporters gathered there. Be sure to visit the James Farm and see where he called home. The newer section of the house was a Sears & Roebuck mail order. Mrs. James decided that the old place was getting too run down—not to mention crowded—and she sent for the two-room addition, assembled on the spot. It still sports the original wallpaper.

This is the famous outlaw's birthplace, the place where his father was hanged and his mother's arm was lost to a Pinkerton's bomb. Enjoy the new on-site museum, which includes a gift shop full of James memorabilia, books, and local crafts, or stick around in August and September for the play, *The Life and Times of Jesse James*. Oh, yes—brother Frank was there, too.

Admission for the museum and home is $4.00 for adults, $3.00 for seniors, and $.75 for children ages six to twelve. Summer hours are from 9:00 A.M. to 4:00 P.M. seven days a week; winter's cold, short days call for slightly reduced hours on weekends: from noon to 4:00 P.M.

On a less grim note, visit the **Claybrook Mansion** across the road from the James Farm. This delightful pre-Civil War home owned by Jesse's daughter and her husband was the last word in modern convenience and elegance. Fairs and historic recreations bring Claybrook alive several times a year. Purchase tickets at the James Farm; the price is included in James Farm tour admission, but it is open only during warm weather; the place is like a barn to heat.

And if you've ever wanted to lay a flower on the outlaw's grave, it's located in Mt. Olivet Cemetery on Highway 92, ½ mile east of Interstate 35 in Kearney (pronounced *CAR-ney*). Look for it near the cedar trees at the west end of the cemetery, which is open during daylight hours year-round.

Legend has it that Jesse, Frank, and/or Cole Younger visited darn near every fallen-down log cabin in this part of Missouri— not to mention the surrounding states. The James gang would have had to be in three places at once, the way their exploits were reported, but no matter. That's the fun thing about legends; they're much more elastic than the truth.

Fast-growing Kearney still hangs on to its small-town charm. At **Clem's Cafe,** 119 East Washington (816–635–4044), Charlie

Davis (not Clem—you'll have to ask Charlie for that story) serves great homemade pies; in fact, everything is homemade. Clem's has really great biscuits-and-gravy and homemade cinnamon rolls, so it is very popular for breakfast around these parts. For good sandwiches try next door at **Charlie's Washington Street Grill** (this time Charlie got his name on it), which is owned by the same folks.

Highway 9 will lead you to the charming little college town of Parkville. This is a bustling crafts and antiques center, with long-time shops interwoven with new establishments. ❖**English Landing,** across the tracks from the old town, houses the **Parkville Fine Arts Gallery** (816–741–7270), a great place to look for original paintings, pottery, or jewelry; the gallery features an "artist of the month," allowing for plenty of variety. In business for over twelve years, it's run by an association of artists. Sort of debunks the "flighty artist" stereotype, doesn't it? Hours are Thursday, Friday, and Saturday 11:00 A.M. until 4:00 P.M.

Just past the shopping complex is quiet English Landing Park on the banks of the Missouri. Look for the historic ninety-three-year-old Waddell "A" truss bridge, one of only two of this type left in the country. It was recently salvaged and moved to its present location. Now it's the focal point of the park, providing a walkway across a small feeder creek leading to the big river.

Cecil Doubenmier is a prize-winning Parkville potter who sells his pottery mostly at craft fairs—there's not room at his place for visitors. If you don't want to follow him around the Midwest, then look for his work at the **Peddler's Wagon,** a downtown quilt shop at 115 North Main (816–741–0225). This little shop sells anything a quilter may need as well as new, handmade quilts and some country gifts. There are also classes in quilting and silk embroidery. Hours are Tuesday through Saturday from 10:00 A.M. until 5:00 P.M.

Cottonwoods and Willows at 112½ Main Street is a cute little shop with a neat assortment of gifts and accessories, unique jewelry, and works of art. The new upstairs shop features kitchen gourmet items and children's clothes and gifts. Hours are 10:00 A.M. to 5:00 P.M. Tuesday through Saturday and noon until 5:00 P.M. on Sunday. Owners are Mary Ann Harvey and Donna Cholak. Call (816) 587–9004 for details.

Of course there is a magnetic attraction when chocolate is mentioned, so you will be irresistibly drawn to **Parkville Coffee & Fudge** at 113 Main Street. Owner Bill Norton has added even more to tempt you, especially if you can resist the siren call of chocolate. Also for sale are items from his, and co-owner Kris Norton's, collection of sporting collectibles—gun shell boxes, duck calls, tobacco tins, decoys, and powder tins—to entice you. Call (816) 587–4200 for more information.

Down to Earth Lifestyles is the quiet eighty-five–acre country place of Bill and Lola Coons just outside of Parkville. It is a contemporary earth-integrated home that gives guests the luxury of total peace and quiet. There are four rooms each with a private bath and color television. You can fish the stocked ponds or swim in an indoor heated pool. Skylights and picture windows allow sunlight and a nice view. The rooms are furnished with country antiques. There are horses, cows, and it is fine for birdwatching. Country breakfasts of omelettes, biscuits, pancakes and country-cured ham and sausage await you in the morning. You can even get breakfast in bed with a flower on the tray and a little bell to ring for extras. It's close to the airport and popular for honeymooners who spend their wedding night here and catch a plane for someplace exotic the next morning. Rooms cost from $65 to $75. Call (816) 891–1018 for reservations and other information.

If you are a devotee of fine baked goods, you'll want to stop by **Fannie's Restaurant** in Platte City (816–431–5675), just across from the recently restored courthouse. Fannie's can serve 150 hungry diners at once, and it's a good thing; busloads of young recruits from Ft. Leavenworth, Kansas, just across the Missouri River, make the trek to taste the cooking that reminds them of home. Homemade bread comes with the meal, or you can buy a giant, fluffy loaf to take home; try the pies, cinnamon rolls, and cobblers as well. Oh, yes, the meals are fine, too. They run from $6.75 to $10.95, or enjoy the smorgasbord on Tuesday, Wednesday, and Thursday—all you can eat for $7.95. Fannie's also features lots of preserves, relishes, and fresh spices from the Amish in Jamesport. Hours are from 8:00 A.M. until 9:00 P.M. Sunday through Thursday, and until 10:00 P.M. on Friday and Saturday.

Just off Highway 45, Weston is a beautiful town tucked between rounded hills, its past shaped as much by the nearby Missouri River and its thread of commerce as by the orchards, vineyards, distilleries, and good tobacco-growing soils here. After the signing of the 1837 Platte Purchase, it attracted settlers who recognized its rich soil—and appreciated the low prices.

Historic preservation in Weston has been a high priority for many years; the place exudes charm as a flower exudes scent. A beautiful old Catholic church overlooks the town, and tobacco and apple barns stand tall on many of the surrounding hills. It has a foursquare flavor that just feels historic—and in fact, Weston bills itself as the Midwest's most historic town. There are over 200 historically significant homes and businesses from before the Civil War alone. Book a tour of the homes (advance reservations are required for the tour; call (816) 640–2650 and ask Marion Gaskill to arrange a mini-tour for you of two of the homes), or visit the **Weston Museum** at Main and Spring streets. Hollywood has discovered Weston, and it's not unknown for movie cameras to roll on Main Street. Recent filming included the Truman movie, *Truman*. Life in Platte County goes way back, long before these neat homes were built or the first still was cranked up; the museum will take you from prehistoric times through World War II. Hours are from 1:00 till 4:00 P.M. Tuesday through Friday, on Saturday until 5:00 P.M., and on Sunday from 1:30 to 5:00 P.M. This one is a bargain; admission is free. Call (816) 386–2977. It's a day trip all by itself.

Weston's ❖ **McCormick Distilling Company** (816–640–2276) is a rare treat, 1¼ miles south of town on Highway JJ. They say this is the oldest continuously active distillery in the country—or at least west of the Hudson River. It was founded in 1856 by stagecoach and Pony Express king Ben Holladay.

Enjoy the fine aroma of strong drink and smokey oak barrels, as you tour the distillery from March though mid-December, Monday through Friday from 9:30 A.M. to 4:00 P.M. or Sunday from 11:00 A.M. till 4:00 P.M.: The tours take about a half hour, and in summer it draws hundreds. The "Ancient Cave" was dug by old Ben himself to store and age his fine product; it's still open to visitors, and in the sultry summer months it's a welcome respite from Missouri heat. The Country Store is open year-round; you can pick up McCormick souvenirs or a gift bottle Monday through Saturday from 9:00 A.M. till 5:00 P.M. or Sundays from 10:00 A.M. till 5:00 P.M. The last tour leaves one-half hour before closing time. Tours are free. Watch those speed bumps on the way in.

137

Weston's newest winery, the **Mission Creek Winery** at highways 45 and P, is open Monday through Saturday from 10:00 A.M. until 6:00 P.M. and from noon until 6:00 P.M. on Sunday. (It is closed Thanksgiving and Christmas). The wines served here are dry and semi-dry made from the vidal, seyval, and catawba grapes. You can buy a gift pack, wine glasses, and T-shirts with the winery's logo to take home to friends. Call (816) 386–5770 for additional details.

Pirtle's Weston Vineyards Winery (816–640–5728) is one of Missouri's most interesting wineries, located in the former German Lutheran Evangelical Church at 502 Spring Street. Jesus made wine, why not Pirtle's? Owner Elbert Pirtle's striking new stained-glass windows depict the winery's logo and a wild rose— the math professor from the University of Missouri at Kansas City is quite the Renaissance man.

Northern Platte County soil is conducive to some fine viticulture; taste the products of these rolling hills Monday through Saturday from 10:00 A.M. to 6:00 P.M. and Sunday noon to 6:00 P.M. The Pirtles love to talk wine and vines. Schedule a wine-tasting party here, and don't forget the mead, a honey-based beverage once thought to be a "love potion." (So what have you got to lose?) It's sweet and smokey—and so it should be, because it's aged in McCormick Distillery oak barrels. Newest in the mead line are sparkling and raspberry mead. Great stuff and just as romantic as the original. They say that originally the church was upstairs and a cooperage was in the basement where barrels were made to serve northwest Missouri.

Across the street at 505 Spring you'll find ❦ **The Vineyards** (816–640–5588). The restaurant features country Continental cuisine and is considered one of the finest places to eat in the Kansas City area. With that reputation, you'd best call for reservations; the place is charming but small, seating only thirty-six . . . well, forty-two in a pinch, if they push the tables together. The kitchen is tucked into every nook and cranny in the basement. Duck, lamb, salmon, and white perch are just some of the featured items on the menu. Appetizers of baked brie with roasted garlic and fresh fruit gives you some idea of the restaurant's continental style. Patio dining during fine weather is a treat. There's a nice mix of art and music in the tiny 1845 Rumpel House. Lunch is served Wednesday through Saturday from 11:00 A.M. until 3:00 P.M. Dinner, however, is served at two seatings, one from 6:00 to 6:30, another from 8:00

to 8:30 P.M. Owner Cheryl Mock says reservations are a must on weekends. There is a Sunday brunch, too.

Just around the corner northwest from the Vineyards is the **American Bowman Restaurant** ("where the Past is Present"), the oldest continuously operating pub in Weston at 150–plus rollicking years old. It offers Irish-style food and entertainment, pewter mugs and kerosene lamps on the tables. There's O'Malley's 1842 Pub, the Post Ordinary, the Heritage Theater, and malt and hops cellars in the same building (as well as an antiques mall).

At Christmas, try the Dickens Dinner; during other seasons, 1837 Dinners, Civil War Dinners, and 19th Century Irish Banquets are yours for the ordering. For reservations call (816) 640–5235. Hours are from 11:30 A.M. until 3:00 P.M. every day but Monday. On Friday and Saturday it reopens for cocktails at 6:30 P.M. and dinner is served at 7:30. Reservations are required.

Steamboat Gothic describes Julie and John Pasley's place, the **Benner House Bed and Breakfast** (816–640–2616) at 645 Main Street (Sierra the dog lives here, too). With its double-deck, wraparound porch and gingerbread trim, the jaunty, turn-of-the-century mansion looks as if it could steam away like the nearby riverboats. Brass beds, baths with pull-chain water closets, and claw-foot tubs add to the interior decor and to your mood. The view from the second floor rooms is spectacular. You can see the wide Missouri across the floodplain. Julie's candlelit breakfasts star cinnamon twists and delightful little pastries filled with cream cheese. A double room costs $65 from January through March and $70 the rest of the year. If you are missing your pets, Sierra the dog will keep you company while you are downstairs. The well-behaved Sierra won't intrude in your room.

Weston Antique Center, 404 North Main, is only one of many great places to shop in town; there are two floors of goodies in three old storefronts, open from 10:00 A.M. to 5:00 P.M. weekdays, 10:00 A.M. to 6:00 P.M. Saturday, and noon to 5:00 P.M. Sunday. Call (816) 640–2664 for more information.

Across the street and upstairs at 511½ Main is **Diddy-Wa-Diddy,** a great and wacky place full of funky sculpture, gifts, pillows, and other goodies. Diddy is worth visiting for its irresistible, one-of-a-kind buys. This is no goose-with-a-raffia-bow place. Call (816) 386–2202 for more details.

The **Missouri Bluffs Boutique & Gallery** is full of quirky, unique clothes, jewelry, and paintings at 512 Main Street (816–640–2770). It's like a maze, with rooms opening off rooms, but the clothing is delightful and the art is worth the search.

If history is your love—and the name Daniel Boone rings a bell—be sure to visit the **Price-Loyles House** just north of Main Street at 718 Spring (816–640–2383). This tidy brick home belonged in the famous Boone family from 1857 to 1989, and all original family furnishings and historic documents were carefully restored and preserved by the present owners. Interestingly, it was mostly the women of the Boone family who owned the home, passing it down from mother to daughter; their delightful furnishings reflect a century and a half of living, but with never a Formica-and-chrome era to be found. They appreciated their heritage and held on to it. You will see the original Victorian beds and clothing, books, the children's room, the old piano—in short, the place looks as if you'd just come to call on a lovely day in the 1800s.

Getting Hungry? Find the **Weston Cafe** at 407 Main Street where the locals eat (along with the visiting film crew here to make a movie about President Harry Truman, appropriately named "Truman"). The Cafe Melt is excellent, and the coffee is plentiful and good. Call (816) 640–5558 for details.

If you're in the mood for something a bit more upscale, the **Avalon,** across the street from the museum, offers an *excellent* beef tenderloin with a bourbon sauce. Kind of a salute to Weston's distillery history, but tender and flavorful as it's possible to be. A little bar area opens onto a charming outdoor courtyard.

Take a short jaunt west of Weston back on Highway 45 to see a view worth going way out of your way for. **Weston Bend State Park** is one of Missouri's newest, and the scenic overlook that spreads a panorama of the Missouri River and rolling fields, wooded loess hills, and Leavenworth clear across the river in Kansas is simply not to be missed. There's also camping, picnicking, hiking, and bicycling, if that's your pleasure. Call (816) 640–5443 for more information.

A bit farther west at the junction of highways 45 and 92 and almost to the bridge to Kansas is the **Beverly Hills Antiques Mall**—in Beverly, definitely not in California. Sure, there are plenty of antiques malls across the state, some better than others. This one's one of the best, with high-quality goods and plenty of variety from fifty-five dealers. No garage sale stuff here, thank you. The mall is open Tuesday through Saturday from 10:00 A.M. to 5:00 P.M. You can't miss it; it's in the old two-story Beverly Lumber Company building, and there's virtually nothing else there—but if you get lost, call (816) 330–3432, and they'll send out the Mounties.

Snow Creek Ski Area (816–386–2200), just north of Weston, is open seven days a week through the cold months. There's plenty of manmade snow (up to 4 feet), lifts, a ski rental, and a cozy lodge for après-ski. Normal costs including equipment rental run $34. (Yes, there is downhill skiing in Missouri; the big hills near the Missouri River are satisfyingly steep, if not long. You can still break a leg if you're so inclined.)

Iatan Marsh near the water treatment plant is the place to be in winter if you're a birder. The warmer waters here attract flocks of migrant waterfowl; who knows what you might spot.

Nearby Bean Lake and Little Bean Marsh catch the birds—and birders—year-round. You may see rails and bitterns, yellow-headed blackbirds, green herons, and egrets along with the ducks and geese. An observation tower makes sighting easier; Little Bean Marsh is the largest remaining natural marsh in Missouri, a remnant of our wetlands heritage.

If you've read Lewis and Clark's journals, you'll remember the description of an oxbow they dubbed "Gosling Lake." This is now thought to be Sugar Lake in Lewis and Clark State Park (816–579–5564), just off Highway 59. There's a huge fish hatchery here; you can see anything from fry to fingerlings to lunkers.

St. Joseph is a river town that lost the race to Kansas City when K.C. was first to bridge the Muddy Mo with the Hannibal Bridge. Still a big and bustling town, it has plenty for the day-tripper to do and see. Consider this: St. Joe has eight, count 'em, eight, museums. The ❖**Albrecht Art Museum** (816–233–7003) has a collection of some of the finest American art in the country, including works by Mary Cassatt, William Merritt Chase, George Catlin, and Missouri's own Thomas Hart Benton. Traveling shows are often exhibited at the Albrecht, including an excellent George Catlin exhibit. Remember Catlin? He's the artist who virtually gave up everything to record the Indian tribes in the early 1800s. It's the best record we have. Housed in an old Georgian manse, the museum at 2818 Frederick has been in operation since 1966. Hours are Tuesday through Friday from 10:00 A.M. to 4:00 P.M. and weekends from 1:00 to 4:00 P.M. Admission is free on Sunday. The rest of the week entry fees are $3.00 for adults, $1.00 for seniors, and students with any type of ID and children under twelve get in free.

Then of course there's the **1858 Patee House.** St. Joseph's only National Historic Landmark, the magnificent old hotel that was the original headquarters for the Pony Express. It houses a tiny village *inside* a downstairs room, plus a steam engine that almost pulls into the rebuilt "station." Also there are the **Jesse James Museum** (816–232–8206), **Roubidoux Row,** and the **Doll Museum.** The **Pony Express Museum** at 914 Penn Street chronicles the history of these early mail runs. Check it out for little more than the price of a stamp ($1.00 for adults and 50 cents for children), April through October from 9:00 A.M. to 5:00 P.M.

There's a morbid fascination to this next one, the ❖**St. Joseph Hospital Psychiatric Museum** (816–387–2300). The museum is housed in an old, rather forbidding wing on the hospital grounds at 3400 Frederick. If you get a little shaky mentally, consider yourself fortunate that it's the 1990s; the museum features twenty display rooms of arcane treatments for psychiatric disorders, from prehistoric times to the recent past. (What did cave men do, you ask? Knocked a hole in your skull to let out the evil spirits. Some patients even lived!) The museum is handicapped accessible, and admission is free.

Missing a museum? It's the **St. Joseph Museum** at Eleventh and Charles streets, founded in 1926. Enjoy displays of North American Indian crafts and Midwestern wildlife as well as the trading post exhibit.

Harding House Bed and Breakfast at 219 North Twentieth Street is a gracious turn-of-the-century home with beveled glass windows, oak woodwork, and many antiques. Hosts Glen and Mary Harding serve tea or sherry by the fire in cool weather and on the porch during the warm months. There's a full American breakfast, topped off with homemade pastries. Rates are from $30 to $35 for a single and from $45 to $40 for a double; each additional person is $10. One grand room has a queen-size bed and rents for $55. For reservations call the River Country B&B service at (314) 771–1993.

Jerre Anne Cafeteria and Bakery (816–232–6585) has

whipped up home-style cooking since 1930; they're good at it. Everything they sell here, they make here. Try the gooseberry pie or the fruit salad pie, originated in the 30s and still sold today to an enthusiastic clientele. The chicken and dumplings is better than Grandma's, and the pork tenderloin is breaded and fried to perfection. They also do a brisk carryout business; the apricot nut bread is wonderful. Jerre Anne's is open Tuesday through Saturday from 11:00 A.M. to 7:00 P.M. at 2640 Mitchell Avenue.

For sheer spectacle, visit ❖ **Squaw Creek National Wildlife Refuge** (816–442–3187) during the fall migration. You may see up to 350,000 snow geese fill the air like clouds. These clouds, though, are full of thunder; the sound of that many wings is deafening. Snow, blue, and Canada geese, migrating ducks and attendant bald eagles (as many as 150 representatives of our national symbol) plus coyote, beaver, muskrat, and deer make this a wildlife-lover's paradise. At least 268 species of birds have been recorded on the refuge. It's an essential stop on the flyway for migratory waterfowl and it has been for centuries; this area was described in the journals of Lewis and Clark. There are now 7,193 acres on the refuge just off Highway 159; watch for signs. Unusual loess hills that look like great dunes, reddish and fantastically eroded, are threaded with hiking trails.

Maryville is home to a gaggle of little antiques shops and malls. Visit **Memory Lane Antique Mall** at 316 East Third (816–582–5990); Hansel's & Gretel, Inc. at 1911 South Main; or **Five Mile Corner Antique Mall** on Highway 71 South (816–562–2294). There's more to do here than just shop, of course. For instance, you can visit the Mary Linn Performing Arts Theater to hear a concert or watch a play performed by the Missouri Repertory Company.

If all this antiques hunting has you ready for a bit of quiet, retreat from the world at ❖ **Conception Abbey** in Conception Junction. Benedictine monks run The Printery House (816–944–2218), where they make greeting cards and colorful notes (ask for their catalog) when they are not going about their real work. Benedictines consider their true work to be prayer—but the work of their hands is prayer, too. Stay over at the 1,000-acre retreat, 900 of which is productive farmland; visit with "the weather monk," or learn along with the seminarians. Call (816) 944–2211 to make a reservation.

As you near Lathrop, your sweet tooth will begin to ache. It's ❦ **Candyman's Mule Barn** (816–528–4263), 600 feet off Interstate 35 at the Lathrop exit. An odd name for a candy place, you say? Owners David and Joan Gessert built their new shop to resemble one of the mule barns that put Lathrop on the map; the town was once the mule capital of America, selling hundreds of these sturdy animals at the turn of the century. Foreign buyers flocked to Lathrop, and nearly all the pack animals for the Boer War were from this little Missouri town. All the barns are gone now, and there's no trace of the busy hotels that housed the buyers; so the Gesserts decided to recreate a bit of history.

Joan's dad started the candy factory over twenty-five years ago, making the best hand-dipped chocolates to come down the pike. The Gesserts do the same; you can watch the kitchen-fresh candy being made daily from 9:00 A.M. to 6:00 P.M. Hours are the same on weekends, but the candy makers get to go home; you'll have to buy without watching. The gift shop also handles other "Best of Missouri Hands" products, including hillbilly bean soup.

If you like the nostalgic feeling of an old-fashioned, wood-floored variety store—the family-style precursor of today's discount giants—you'll love **McCullough Variety** at 619 Oak Street in Lathrop (816–740–3612). As owners Regina and Donald Moore say, "You name it, we have it." Hours are 9:00 A.M. to 5:00 P.M. Monday through Friday and on Saturday they "close about three."

In Plattsburg, Shirley and John Grant's **Curiosity Corner** (816–539–2666) specializes in silver, coins, tools, and furniture at 216 North Main. **Tiques & Stuff** (816–539–3232) is Charles and Michele Spease's place on the east side of the courthouse at 108 Maple. It is open Monday through Saturday from 10:00 A.M. to 5:00 P.M.

There is also a bed and breakfast in town. **Charlotte's Apple Blossom Inn** at the corner of Broadway and 2nd Street has private baths and offers a full breakfast (and a traditional apple dessert). Call (816) 539–3243 for reservations.

Smithville is near the intersection of highways 169 and 92, and if all you know about the place is that it used to flood, you're in for a nice surprise. The town is close by the new Smithville Lake for summer fun, and there are plenty of shops to browse in.

Squaw Creek National Wildlife Refuge

❖ **Smithville Lake** is a fairly recent addition to Missouri's array of man-made lakes. Constructed by the U.S. Army Corps of Engineers to control flooding that Smithville residents have lived with since there was a Smithville, the lake is also a magnet for water-lovers. Turn north off Highway 92 (between Kearney and the town of Smithville) for sailing, fishing, boating, or just messing around.

Also at the lake is Missouri's own **Woodhenge,** a re-creation of a Woodland Indian site that may have been used as an astronomical observatory around 5,000 years ago. The original location of Woodhenge was uncovered during the building of the lake, and dredging was halted until archaeologists could study the area. It was important enough that the present site was reconstructed as an aid to further study; scientists from Woods Hole, Massachusetts, have come here to observe the solstice and equinox.

Near the new dam at Smithville Lake one of the largest glacial erratics in the area squats like a patient dinosaur under an accre-

145

tion of graffiti. A large, pink Sioux-quartzite stone, this elephant-sized monster was brought here by the last glacier some 15,000 years ago. It may have been an important landmark for the Paleo-Indians who lived in the area.

At the Jerry Litton Visitors' Center (816–532–0174), also near the dam, you can find out about these earliest inhabitants, about visits by Lewis and Clark as they came through on the nearby Missouri River, about the pioneer settlers, and about the birds and animals that make this area home. Admission is free.

About 3½ miles north of Smithville on Highway 169, you can turn right on Highway W and drive 2 miles across the east side of the lake to Paradise. This community is home to about twenty-five families and **Ed Gilliam's Shop.** Gilliam carves Father Christmas, some sixty-seven styles of Santas, and, coincidentally, looks as though he should be surrounded by elves himself. Perhaps it is because he was born on Christmas Day. Ed has been carving since he was twelve years old—that's over fifty years now—and still fills his shop with piles of Missouri and Minnesota basswood, sugar pine, cottonwood bark, and driftwood bits that drop from the hundreds of carvings lining the shop. Santas of every style line the walls. There are fat Santas and thin Santas, Black Santas and Uncle Sam Santas. Or how about a German Belznickle, a rather stern-looking Santa who carries a switch.

They are not all Santas, though. Ed turns out cigar store Indians, folk art, cowboys, and all manner of Americana ranging from 4 inches to 4 feet in height. Ed is usually at his house in Paradise, but it is a good idea to call first, (816) 873–2592. To find Ed's house find Clyde's General Store, a two-story brick building, then turn right at the end of the building and go two blocks to Holmes Street. Ed's place is at 18403 Holmes Street.

NORTHEAST MISSOURI

26

9

8

Mark Twain's
River

Glaciated Plains

25 22 23 27

24

28

7 6
5

4

21
Bluffs of the
Mighty Mo

17 16
20 19 18

Antiques &
Antiquity
3

Missouri's
Monarchy

29 30

Northern
Wineries
15 14
13 12 11

2 1

10

1. The Mother-in-Law House
2. The Elvis Is Alive 50s Cafe and Museum
3. Lock and Dam No. 25
4. Orthwein Mansion Bed and Breakfast
5. Fresh Ayers
6. Hammon Glass
7. Garth Woodside Mansion
8. Golden Eagle Riverboat Dinner Theatre
9. Sheffler Rock Shop and Geode Mine
10. Bethel
11. Daniel Boone's Home
12. Mount Pleasant Wine Company
13. Nona Woodworks
14. Blumenhof Vineyards and Winery
15. Concord Hill Bed and Breakfast

16. Museum of Art and Archaeology
17. Over the Edge
18. Carol Leigh's Specialties
19. Trattoria Strata Nova
20. Les Bourgeois Winery
21. Henderson's
22. General John J. Pershing Boyhood Home
23. Andrew Taylor Still National Osteopathic Museum
24 Thousand Hills State Park
25. The Pear Tree
26. Mark Twain Birthplace State Historic Site
27. Ruffles and Lace
28. Chance Gardens
29. Winston Churchill Memorial and Library
30. Graham Cave State Park

NORTHEAST MISSOURI

North of St. Louis, the land changes. Hills are gentler; they are the legacy of a wall of glacial ice that smoothed rough edges and brought with it tons of rich, deep soil some 15,000 years ago. Thanks to that gift, quintessentially Mid-American towns are dotted with the docile shapes of cows; barns are large and prosperous-looking; fence rows blossom with wildflowers; and bluebirds and meadowlarks sing.

Northeast Missouri is rich in history as well. That consummate storyteller Mark Twain was born here; he has endowed us with more colorful quotations than any writer before or since. You've heard of Mark Twain Cave and his boyhood home in Hannibal, but did you know that near Florida, Missouri, you can explore Samuel Clemens's birthplace? General Omar Bradley's birthplace is in this area, too, along with General John J. Pershing's boyhood home and a monument to General Sterling Price. (Generally speaking, it seems to be a great place for great men.)

The Civil War raged from St. Louis to the Iowa border, where the Battle of Athens took place. Tiny Palmyra was the site of an atrocity that presidents Abraham Lincoln and Jefferson Davis called the worst of war crimes.

All along the Missouri River valley are tiny, picturesque towns, many with a German heritage, and many with wineries where you may taste the best the United States has to offer. (Mt. Pleasant's Port won the gold in international competition.) Lewis and Clark passed by these town sites on their way to the Northwest Passage and remarked on them in their journals.

The mighty Mississippi is busy with commerce, as it has been for more than 200 years. Barges churn by, and the power of that mile-wide channel vibrates under you as you stand on a riverboat's deck. The Great River Road, which runs along the Mississippi from New Orleans to its source, is so picturesque that plans are afoot to make it a National Scenic Roadway.

Bald eagles feed along both rivers in winter, drawn by open water and good fishing below the locks and dams. Amish communities, college towns, museums, eateries, petroglyphs, wildlife refuges—whatever your interest, you'll find it satisfied in northeast Missouri, where literally everything is off the beaten path.

ANTIQUES AND ANTIQUITY

Just north of St. Louis is St. Charles. The first capitol of Missouri is located at 208–216 South Main Street (314–946–9282); legislators met here until October 1826, when the abandoned buildings began to settle slowly into decay. In 1961 the state of Missouri began a ten-year restoration project that sparked the revitalization of St. Charles. Shops, restaurants, and delightful little surprises abound. Take a walking tour of history; the St. Charles Convention and Visitors' Bureau (314–946–7776) can get you started.

St. Charles' **Boone's Lick Trail Inn,** (314–947–7000) is the only B&B in St. Charles. The city is the state's largest National Register Historic District with 10 blocks of mid-1800s buildings authentically restored. Stroll along cobblestone streets, watch the river flow by, enjoy fine dining, antiquing, and history.

If your sweet tooth kicks in and you've a dime or two in your pocket, satisfy that craving the old-fashioned way at **Pop's General Store,** 322 South Main (314–723–6040). Imagine an old-style emporium with a potbellied stove, brass cash register, and advertising memorabilia from soap powders to nostrums; that place is here. Richard House (otherwise known as Pop) sacks horehound candy, peppermint drops, and other old favorites by the pound or by the piece.

With your sweet tooth satisfied, you can head for the riverboat and some casino fun.

Both of our big rivers claimed more than their share of casualties. Steamboats sank with dismal regularity, and to this day— locks and dams notwithstanding—riverboat captains watch their charts and take their soundings much as Samuel Clemens did when he sang out, "Mark twain." The channels of both the Missouri and the Mississippi are graveyards for boats from tugs to stern-wheelers; the rivers are not to be taken lightly. Our Lady of the Rivers Shrine, a lighthouse-like monument at Portage de Sioux, is a reminder that brave travelers needed all the help they could get. That said, it's time to board at **The Spirit of Saint Charles River Front Station** (314–940–4300). The station is off I-70 just ten minutes west of Lambert Airport and gives you two action-packed casinos. The casino on the boat is open from 9:00 A.M. until 5:00 P.M. seven days a week with two-hour-long gaming sessions. The late night sessions at 1:00 and 2:00 A.M. are

149

three hours long. The riverboat boards every odd hour beginning at 9:00 A.M. and cruises only during daylight hours depending on the weather and river conditions. There is a $2.00 per person gaming tax. Casino St. Charles on the riverfront, starts sessions on even hours beginning at 10 A.M. Take the Sixth Street exit (229a) just across the bridge.

◆ **The Mother-in-Law House** at 500 South Main must first have its name explained. In 1866, a French bride so missed her mother that her understanding husband built her a home with a dividing wall down the center so his mother-in-law could come to America and move in with them. Donna Hafer found the red-brick beauty on Main Street in the historic district of St. Charles and gave it the TLC it needed to become the gracious, antiques-filled restaurant it is today. The dining room has the original oil lamps. Glittering prisms pour a soft glow on the antique furnishings. Fresh flowers adorn each table and the staff wears dainty pinafores. The recipes have been in Donna's family for over a century and make the salad bar a delight. Her coconut cream pie is renowned in the area.

The restaurant is open for lunch Monday through Saturday and for dinner Tuesday through Saturday. Hours are Tuesday through Saturday with lunch from 11:00 A.M. until 2:00 P.M. and dinner from 5:30 to 10:00 P.M. Monday is lunch only. Reservations are recommended; call (314) 946–9444.

◆ **Elvis is Alive 50s Cafe and Museum** at I–70 and Main Street in Wright City is a shrine to the King. A Cadillac that Elvis rode in is parked out front, and inside the cafe you can join owner Bill Beeny and eat all of the strange food Elvis made famous—like a fried peanut butter and banana sandwich. This little spot features an audiotape supposedly made after Elvis' death. There is a replica of his tomb at Graceland and a video called "The Elvis Files," which denies his death. Cafe hours are from 8:00 A.M. until 9:00 P.M. Bill even has a chapel for those of you who want to get married there (find your own Justice of the Peace, however). Of course, there is a large gift shop. Museum hours are 9:00 A.M. to 5:00 P.M. The museum is free; donations are accepted. Call (314) 745–3154 for more information.

Winfield, Clarksville, Louisiana—the names are strung like beads along the Great River Road (now Scenic Highway 79) between St. Louis and Hannibal. These little towns harbor more antiques shops than you know what to do with. There are so many, in fact, that we only have room to include those towns that have additional attractions. Don't let that stop you, though; Missouri is a mecca for affordable goodies. If you can't find what you're looking for, you just haven't found the magic spot yet, and isn't the search as much fun as the finding?

◆ **Lock and Dam No. 25** on the Mississippi is a fine place to watch the eagles feed in the winter. Or take the old Winfield Ferry across the river to Calhoon County, Illinois. (Don't worry, you can come right back if you're not through antiques hunting.)

If you fancy a bit of wilderness about now, a short detour west on Highway 47 will take you to spectacular **Cuivre River State Park** (314–528–7247). More than 31 miles of trails will let you discover one of the state's most rustic parks. The rough terrain is more like the Ozarks than the rest of glacier-smoothed northern Missouri, and like the Ozarks, it encourages many plants only found farther south such as flowering dogwood, Missouri orange coneflower, and dittany. Frenchman's Bluff overlooks the Cuivre River Valley. The Lincoln Hills region, where Cuivre River State Park is found, formed millions of years ago when intense pressures caused the earth to buckle. Erosion cut even deeper; the resulting springs, sinkholes, and rocky cliffs make this an outdoor-lover's paradise. Archaeologists speculate that the region was home to prehistoric humans as early as 12,000 years ago; a 1937 dig unearthed a stone chamber containing a skeleton and pieces of a clay pot.

Clarksville is finding its way back—but back toward the past. With about the same population that it had in 1860, this spick-and-span town has new life in its old veins. A historic preservation effort mounted in 1987 has saved many of the delightful buildings in record time. One of those buildings is the Clifford Banking Company, now an antiques store, where you'll find furniture and accessories from 10:00 A.M. to 5:00 P.M. most days. Next door is the Front Street Gallery, a co-op comprised of artists from St. Charles to the Hannibal area. Other downtown commercial buildings, homes, and churches have already been restored, and more are under way. Plenty of other antiques stores are nearby; ask at Clifford's.

The **Clifford Wirick Centennial House** at 105 South Second Street (314–242–3376) is on the National Register of

Historic Places. If you love stained glass—old or new—you'll find this place to your liking. They also do repairs if you have a favorite piece that needs attention. Owner/historian Vernon Hughes is here to answer your questions about Clarksville or provide you with fine examples of American dinnerware, glass, china, pottery, and prints. The house is open from 10:00 A.M. till 5:00 P.M. most days.

The town commands an 800–square-mile view of the valley of the Big Muddy from an aerie on the highest point overlooking the Mississippi. Surprisingly, barge traffic on the river below is constant—you don't expect to see so much action. See ice-formed drumlins (those are hills) in this panoramic view from Look-Out Point, 600 feet above the river. This is one place you probably won't want to climb so take the skylift.

Up top, check out the country store; you'll find folk art, country cooking, home-style candy, and souvenirs. The kids can let off some of the steam they've built up in the back of the van all day. There are a jungle gym, video games, and a wonderful tilted house.

Clarksville is a great place to observe wintering eagles; the Missouri Department of Conservation's Eagle Days, held here the last weekend of January, can swell the town's normal population of 500 to over 5,000. Is it worth it? You bet it is. Even the *New York Times* visited to check out the approximately 350 bald eagles. The Great River Road Visitors' Center offers information, a museum, and spanking-clean restrooms.

In Louisiana, you'll come face to face with temptation—if you're an antiques nut, that is. **Jeanne's House of Antiques** (314–754–6836), one block east of the highway on Virginia Street, is open every day from 10:00 A.M. to 5:00 P.M. There are twenty rooms stuffed with everything from china and silver (you could set an elegant, although eclectic, table from your finds) to lovely old quilts, stoneware, primitives, and crafts. The building's a kick, too. It's a huge mansion with a wraparound porch and big windows that let in the light.

It's not all just antiques and eats in Louisiana; if you're a history buff, you'll enjoy the Georgia Street Historic District, where the ❖ **Orthwein Mansion Bed and Breakfast,** a baronial manse, offers pure class. It was featured in *Midwest Living, St. Louis,* and *Ozark Airlines* magazines. Reservations are made through River Country Bed and Breakfast, (314–771–1993).

MARK TWAIN'S RIVER

For tourists, Hannibal is not exactly "off the beaten path." Half a million people annually come through this picturesque little town. Everybody knows about the Mark Twain Boyhood Home. Everybody's seen that fence—or at least pictures of it—where Tom Sawyer tricked his buddies into doing his work for him. (The original fence was 9 feet tall and a lot longer than the one that stands here now—no wonder the kid didn't want to paint it by himself.) You may even know about Margaret Tobin Brown's home (remember the *Unsinkable Molly Brown?*), the Molly Brown Dinner Theater, and the fine dinner cruise on the Mississippi riverboat, the *Mark Twain*. So we'll let you find them on your own—it's easy.

While you're in the historic district, though, look for **Ayers Pottery.** Steve Ayers does beautiful work, primarily using Missouri clays, and the shop is set up to encourage your involvement. There's a hall around three sides of the workshop, so you can see every step in the process. He also stocks a selection of beautiful kites, porcelain jewelry, baskets, and hand-forged things—goodies he picks up while on the craft-show circuit.

Even when Steve's out of town, the shop is open at 308 North Third, seven days a week in the summer from 8:00 A.M. to 6:00 P.M. (314–221–6960). It's only one-half-block from the Mark Twain Museum. Steve has recently opened another shop, aptly named ◆ **Fresh Ayers** at 213 North Main Street (314–221–1017) where, along with pottery, Steve also carries coffee beans in many flavors. If you want to try some of them, there is a delightful cappuccino bar in the back of the store. Steve is involved in a project to list all of the artists living along the river route. While you sip your espresso, Steve can give you directions to many other craftspeople to visit along the way.

One of the first places you will find is ◆ **Hammon Glass** nearby at 115 Hill Street. It is the shop of John Miller, a third-generation glass blower who grew up tending the furnaces for his uncle and grandfather. His shop is in a former bottling plant, all concrete and perfect for his trade. John's grandfather blew lamp chimneys, communion glasses and railroad globes and

Garth Woodside Mansion

functional glassware back when it wasn't so much an art as a functional craft. His father grew up working in a glass shop. Drop by the shop and look at the unique items he makes now. Marbles are his biggest seller, believe it or not, but there is a wonderful collection of perfume bottles, paperweights, and oil lamps as well as striking free-form sculptures. Of course there are glasses and bowls, candy dishes and all manner of beautiful glassware. Call (314) 221–3900 for more information.

If elegant Victoriana is your weakness, stay in gingerbread heaven at the ❖ **Garth Woodside Mansion.** This one's on the National Register, and it deserves to be. Mark Twain was often a guest of the Garths.

You won't believe the three-story flying staircase with no visible means of support; you might not trust it, either, though they say it's quite safe. Enter the walnut-lined library through 9–foot doors, or check out the extra-wide hostess's seat in the dining room (no, the hostess wasn't that wide; it accommodated the voluminous petticoats of the era). Rates are from $65 to $105. Call (314) 221–2789 for more information.

Innkeepers Irv and Diane Feinberg go all out. For large tour groups they will arrange a tea and tour, complete with hot or iced tea (according to season) and Victorian-style goodies. The mansion is in a beautiful country setting—thirty-nine acres of meadows and woodlands that retain the feel of early Hannibal countryside.

Don't miss the mansion where Mr. Clemens addressed the cream of Hannibal society on his last visit here in 1902. It's **Rockcliffe Mansion** (314–221–4140), at 1000 Bird Street, a wonderfully quirky place full of Art Nouveau decor, which was a breakaway style from the established Victorian. It, too, is on the National Register of Historic Places.

There are guided tours daily from March through November, 9:30 A.M. till 5:00 P.M., and from December through February, 11:30 A.M. till 3:30 P.M. There's a small admission charge.

Look . . . there, by the side of the road. A riverboat's run aground! Well, not really, but it sure looks that way. The ◆ **Golden Eagle Riverboat Dinner Theatre** (314–288–5273) at Canton was built where she sits, firmly at anchor in Missouri's rich, alluvial soil. It's one of the state's most unusual businesses, to say the least. It will put you in mind of the old diners shaped like a coffeepot or a hot dog (at the risk of sounding irreverent).

This landlocked beauty inside the Canton levee at Second and Green streets incorporates many authentic bits of riverboat memorabilia. The Grand Salon is modeled after the finest old packets ever to steam up the Muddy Mississip.

Don't miss the live entertainment. There are musical comedies, melodramas, and vaudeville reviews featuring members of the Showboat Company. And just because this eagle is landlocked doesn't mean there's no calliope. The sound of a steam calliope seems wedded to these steam-powered boats, since the music was powered by the same hot vapor that drove the engines. Owner and producer Captain Dave Steinbeck puts on one heck of a concert each evening during the summer months.

If you've just got to get out on that river, the Canton Ferry, owned by Mr. and Mrs. Wallace Kiser, will whisk you over and back. There's been a ferry in continuous operation here since 1853.

If you're at all Irish (and who isn't, at least one day of the year), don't miss St. Patrick, the only town in the world (with a post office) named for everybody's patron saint. If you like, send a package of mail containing stamped, addressed envelopes to Postmaster Mike Lewis, St. Patrick, MO 63466, to get the special St. Paddy's Day cancellation.

It's more fun to visit the post office, though. The letter boxes are antique, and the hospitality is the old-fashioned kind you'd expect in a town of fourteen souls. Hours are 9:00 A.M. till 1:00 P.M.

The Shrine of St. Patrick is fashioned after the Church of Four Masters in Donegal, Ireland; the style is ancient Celtic. There's a round bell tower with a circular staircase of the kind used on the Auld Sod. Dublin-made stained-glass windows are patterned after the famous illuminated manuscript, the *Book of Kells*; the most unusual has St. Patrick surrounded by the symbols of Ireland's four provinces: Ulster, Leinster, Munster, and Connaught. Perhaps you are beginning to catch the flavor of the place.

Oh, yes, there's another unusual attraction: geodes. What's a geode, you may ask? You must not be a rock hound, if you are wondering. A geode is a rather undistinguished blob that looks like a rounded river rock. But inside—ah, inside—there is magic. Beautiful crystal formations fill the hollow center of a geode like a Fabergé egg; they're considered gemstones.

Some of the world's finest geodes are found in this small area. You can buy one at Buschling Place 3 miles north of Dempsey; the Buschlings specialize in country crafts, turquoise, and, of course, geodes. Or you can find your own at ❖ **Sheffler Rock Shop and Geode Mine** (816–754–6443), located at the junction of Highway 61 and the Highway 136 Spur, from April to December. This is the only geode mine in the U.S. that is registered with the Federal Bureau of Mines. Watch for the round rock building made entirely of sixty tons of mineral specimens. This shop is open year-round and has been selling minerals, agates, and jewelry-making supplies for more than thirty years. If you come to dig your own geode, bring a rock hammer and a bit of muscle; these treasures don't come without sweat equity.

❖ **Bethel** is the kind of place you dream about when you're feeling nostalgic for "the good old days" when things were simpler, and the world was more easily understood, when people could meet one another's eyes directly and a handshake meant everything. Bethel old-timers say, "When you get it right, why change?" And here, they've pulled it off.

It's not all old-time ambience and down-home goodies. Bethel has a thriving art colony. The town plays host to frequent festivals, workshops, and seminars celebrating its agricultural, cultural, and social heritage throughout the year. Thousands of people flock here for the World Sheep and Wool Festival (ouch! a pun!). Other festivals throughout the year draw folks for antiques, fiddlers, music, and Christmas in Bethel. If you see a line on the sidewalk downtown, likely it's for the family storefront bakery that only opens during festivals. Breads, cinnamon rolls—they've got it. Get in line!

Founded as a utopian religious colony in 1844, the whole town is listed on the National Register of Historic Places. The museum can fill you in on the details; it's open daily.

Bethel is friendly; you're family as soon as you arrive. And it's best to arrive hungry. The **Fest Hall Restaurant** (816–284–6493) serves "good food and plenty of it," the folks say, at reasonable family prices. They also serve homemade pies that make it worth jettisoning a diet for, seven days a week. Hours are from 6:00 A.M. until about 8:00 P.M.

If you want to stay over, the **Bethel German Colony Bed and Breakfast** (same telephone number as Fest Hall) welcomes visitors to four rooms furnished in a simple country style above the Colony Restaurant. Incredibly affordable rates of $15 per person include a country breakfast blessed with home-baked bread and the Fest Hall's own apple butter. (Close your eyes. Imagine the rich, sweet aroma of bubbling apples and spices in an old copper kettle. That's what goes on your breakfast muffins.) If the restaurant is closed when you arrive, pop over to the grocery store on the corner for room keys.

NORTHERN WINERIES

Take a different loop to see the Missouri River and the little wineries that sprout like vines along its banks. There's a lot of history along the Missouri; whatever your interest, you'll find plenty to see and do.

Take Highway 94, for example. It's for people who don't like their roads straight and flat: mile after mile of two-lane blacktop that curves and winds from St. Charles to Jefferson City. It is one of the most beautiful and exhilarating drives in the state and is a practical route to mid-Missouri for those of us who don't enjoy the mind-numbing 65 mph of the interstate. Since you have this book with you, the assumption can be made that you like to drive, so Highway 94 is a "must-do" trip. Cross Interstate 40 outside St. Charles, go a mile, and turn into the August A. Busch Memorial Wildlife Area. This 7,000–acre preserve has nature trails, hunting areas, shooting ranges, and thirty-two lakes for fishing. It features a self-guided tour of native prairie, pine plantation, and farming practices that benefit wildlife. In the spring and fall, thousands of migrating birds can be seen at the shorebird and waterfowl preserve.

Missouri River State Trail, Missouri's part of the KATY Trail following the old MKT Railroad right-of-way, meanders through here, and on weekends large crowds of bikers and hikers wander along the 26 miles of trail from Highway 40 at Weldon Springs to Marthasville. If you have a bike on the roof, there is convenient parking all along the trail. There are plenty of places to get a meal or rent bikes if you didn't bring your own. There's even a bed and breakfast and a winery for a picnic lunch along the trail.

There's a spectacular view of the river beyond the outskirts of St. Louis on Interstate 70. There are so many good destinations along this route that you don't have to tell anyone that you are on it because you like to hug the corners and push the federally mandated speed limit to its max. This road will challenge the best Grand Prix wannabe with its collection of diamond-shaped signs warning of another set of sharp curves. But slow down and watch for wild turkey and deer. Enjoy the tidy farmhouses and pretty churches as you aim for towns like Augusta, Dutzow, and Hermann that wait along the route.

You will enjoy Defiance's antiques shops and the Carpenter's Love, a woodworking shop right on the KATY Trail. History buffs will want to take a 6–mile detour from Highway 94 down Highway F to the Daniel Boone home.

Somehow you would imagine a log cabin—or a sod hut, maybe. This beautiful stone house with ivy clinging to its double chimneys, crisply painted shutters, and ample back porch is not what you'd expect at all. ◆ **Daniel Boone's Home** at Defiance is ruggedly elegant and comfortable. Add a VCR and a microwave, and you could move in tomorrow. Boone lived to a ripe old age. The naturalist John James Audubon described him as a "stout, hale, hearty man."

Here are Daniel's powder horn and his long rifles, his writing desk, and the very bed where his long career on the American frontier ended. It's a small bedchamber; the four-poster bed looks as if it were just made up with fresh sheets and a clean white counterpane, ready for the man himself to come in from a hard day of hunting, settling the frontier, and making history.

The kitchen is cozy, with low beams and a huge fireplace. Mrs. Boone's butter churn sits nearby, and you can almost see the family gathered here, waiting expectantly for that rich, yellow butter to spread on hearth-baked bread. A chapel, summer kitchen and spool house have been added on the grounds and more buildings are planned.

Tours are given daily, March through December, from 9:00 A.M. to 6:00 P.M. Call (314) 987–2221 for more information.

Leaving Defiance, you'll enter the Missouri River Valley wine region. There are more wineries along Highway 94 than anywhere else in the state. You can visit **Boone Country Winery** west of Defiance, **Montelle Winery** at Osage Ridge, **Augusta Winery** and Mount Pleasant Wine Company in Augusta, and Blumenhof Vineyards in Dutzow. All offer wine tasting and sales as well as great spots to enjoy a bottle of wine with a picnic lunch.

Just down the road apiece from Dan'ls house you'll find the little German wine-producing town of Augusta. A hundred and fifty years ago it was a self-sufficient town with a cooperage works, stores, and a German school. Before Prohibition, when Missouri was the second-largest wine-producing state in the nation, there were thirteen wineries located in Augusta's valley, beyond the bluffs above the southernmost bend of the river. Deep, well-drained soil and freedom from spring frosts were perfect for viticulture. This is recognized as America's first official wine district and the first in the New World to bear an official "Appellation Control" designation.

Augusta still deserves its reputation. **❖Mount Pleasant Wine Company** (314–228–4419) was purchased in 1966 by Lucian and Eva Dressel (it's now owned by MPW, Inc). A short twenty years later, the Dressels' 1986 Vintage Port took top port honors in the International Wine and Spirit Competition in London, England, making theirs the first Missouri winery since

Mount Pleasant Wine Company

Prohibition to win an international gold medal, from a field of 1,175 wines and more than twenty countries.

Mount Pleasant's 1987 Jour de la Victoire Ice Wine also won a silver medal, the highest award given to an American ice wine. The Cheese Wedge, on-site at the winery, features products made in Missouri. You can buy cheese from Emma (that's a town), sausage from Washington, and mustard from Wolf Island, Missouri. Hours are Monday through Saturday from 10:00 A.M. to 5:00 P.M. and Sunday from noon to 5:30 P.M. Mount Pleasant even delivers!

Gleaming copper and brass, the work of more than thirty potters and craftspeople, greet your eyes at **Americana Galleries** (314–228–4494) a cluster of reconstructed early log buildings. Coppersmith Michael Bruckdorfer keeps random winter hours, but is open from April through Christmas on weekdays from 10:30 A.M. to 4:30 P.M., Saturdays from 10:00 A.M. to 5:00 P.M., and Sunday afternoons. The galleries are at the corner of Walnut and Ferry streets.

The town invites leisurely exploration. Stay over at the **Lindenhoff Country Inn** (314–228–4617) at the corner of Walnut and Jackson; you can't miss that pink Victorian with its blue trim and ornate iron fence. The rate is $65 ($75 on weekends) double occupancy per night. Hostess Mary Peters says that Bethel is "one of the cutest towns, and only an hour from St. Louis." Other B&Bs are nearby; look around.

If you love fine furniture with an elegant, contemporary feel, you'd hardly expect to find it in the backcountry. But at ◆**Nona Woodworks,** furniture maker Michael Bauermeister is full of surprises. He works with Missouri woods to create delicate, finely designed pieces that would grace the best of homes. "Rita's Desk," for example, is a lovely little fall-front desk of cherry wood. The angular top is a beautiful contrast to the curved and hard-carved legs.

Michael's shop is in an old-fashioned store building in the town of Nona, which isn't a town anymore. It's just Michael's house and shop and a few other buildings. Follow High Street west, which turns into Augusta Bottom Road, 3 miles to the shop on the left side of the road. The shop is just 3 miles from Mt. Pleasant Winery. Shop hours are unpredictable because special orders and commissions keep the craftsman hopping. Call (314) 228–4663 to make sure your trip won't be for nothing.

A one-lane bridge followed by a ninety-degree turn leads you to Dutzow. (If you found Augusta charming, Dutzow is downright quaint.) This historic Dutch town, founded in 1832 by Baron Von Bock, was the first German settlement in the Missouri River Valley. In the mid-nineteenth century "Missouri's Rhineland" attracted immigrants who were inspired by enthusiastic accounts of natural beauty and bounty; among the most convincing was Gottfried Duden's *Report on a Journey to the Western States of North America,* published in 1829, which contributed to the settlement of these lovely little enclaves all up and down the Missouri River. The town offers several antiques shops and a pretty good sandwich at the **Dutzow Deli** in an old gas station next to the town post office. It's a popular stop along the KATY Trail. Hours are 9:00 A.M. to 7:00 P.M. Monday through Thursday, 9:00 A.M. until 10:00 P.M. on Friday (but the grill closes at 8:00 P.M.) and from 9:00 A.M. until 6:00 P.M. on Saturday and Sunday.

The severe floods of 1993 and 1995 were setbacks for KATY

Trail State Park, which runs along the river for more than 200 miles. This long, skinny state park snakes along connecting towns from St. Louis to Sedalia. Completed portions are at each end and work is continuing between them. The finely crushed gravel trail allows biking or hiking for 45 miles from St. Charles west to Treloar. You cross bottomland forests filled with migratory birds, wetlands, fields of wildflowers, and dolomite bluffs. The small towns along the way welcome trail users. You can stop for wine tastings at Defiance and Marthasville and lunch at Augusta.

◆**Blumenhof Vineyards and Winery** (314–433–2245) takes its name from the Blumenberg family's ancestral farm in the Harz Mountains of Germany; *blumenhof* translates as "court of flowers." Enjoy the winery's Teutonic decor and the welcome invitation to stop and smell the flowers—along with the bouquet of the wine. Blumenhof produces wines from the finest American and European varietal grapes. There's a full range of wines, but dry table wines are a tour de force. (The Vidal Blanc won a gold medal in international competition.) Visit any day except Easter, Thanksgiving, Christmas, or New Year's, 10:30 A.M. to 5:30 P.M. Monday through Saturday and from noon to 5:30 P.M. on Sunday.

The ◆**Concord Hill Bed and Breakfast** (314–932–4228) offers city-weary guests three large bedrooms and a huge loft that comfortably sleeps five adults. Add a hot tub, wet bar, and full kitchen; it's an ideal weekend retreat for groups of up to eleven. A continental breakfast is provided and anything from elegant candlelight dinners to simple box lunches can be pre-arranged; now that's a getaway. This nineteenth-century farmhouse is in the tiny agricultural town of Concord Hill, population forty; this is definitely off the beaten path! Rooms cost $75 for two guests.

Charrette Creek Winery at 304 Depot Street is new to Marthasville. Owner Joe Meiners has created quite a place for tasting Missouri wines. His place is practically right on the KATY Trail; hikers and bikers can relax in air conditioned comfort on hot days, or warm up on cold days. Meiners not only has wine in the Scarlett O'Hara room, but there's a deli for putting together a picnic lunch on the patio. Now about the Scarlett O'Hara room: The back bar is the original one from *Gone With The Wind*, "they say," according to Joe. So if you want to taste some of Joe's creations, wines with romantic names like Osage Mist (a semisweet wine) or Summer Blush made from Missouri's vidal, seyval, cynthiana, or vignole grapes, this is a good place to do it. And, if it happens to be a Saturday or Sunday, you can hear live jazz from 2:00 until 5:00 P.M. Winery hours are from 11:00 A.M. until 5:00 P.M. seven days a week. Look for the intersection of Highways 94/47/D. Call (314) 433-5859 for more information.

There is one more KATY stop at Marthasville. "Over the river and through the woods, to Grandmother's house we go...." If you don't have a grandma in the country, visit **Gramma's House** (314-433-2675) near Marthasville; it's like going home. Enjoy a brisk game of horseshoes, look for a bluebird on the fence, or just skip stones in the creek. After sleeping like a stone in these peaceful surroundings, your "grandma"—that is, hostess—will fix you a hearty breakfast; best clean your plate. Weekend rates are $75 per couple; two lovely private cottages are $90. Hosts Jim and Judy Jones are delighted with the cottages called the Smokehouse and the Playhouse. Both have fireplaces, but the Playhouse has a huge bathtub in front of the fireplace for a romantic bubblebath à *deux*. Gramma's House is popular with trail users; make this Gramma's a rest stop and stay on for the comfort and the ambience.

BLUFFS OF THE MIGHTY MO

Highway 94 winds over steep hills set with ponds and quiet, picturesque farms. Small and almost picture-postcard pretty buildings nestled in the trees are clearly visible in winter and half-hidden in summer; you'll have to look sharp. The highway follows the river through a series of tiny towns that give you a taste of Missouri past. Rhineland, Bluffton, Steedman, Mokane—each is as inviting as the last. Heads up; you may find a great little cafe here or a hidden mine of antiques.

Plan to stay a while in Columbia. It's a great base camp for some far-flung exploring—that is, once you can tear yourself away from the town itself.

Columbia is home of the University of Missouri, a beautiful campus that houses a number of disciplines. If you have an interest in antiquities, don't miss the ◆**Museum of Art and Archaeology,** boasting a collection from six continents and five millennia. The museum, in Pickard Hall at the corner of University Avenue and Ninth Street, is on the historic Francis quadrangle. Built in 1894, it's on the National Register of Historic Places. You'll find artworks by Lyonel Feininger, Lakshmi, Francken the Younger, and many well-known classical and contemporary American artists. The museum is open 9:00 A.M. till 5:00 P.M. Tuesday through Friday and noon till 5:00 P.M. on weekends.

Archaeology has long been a strong field of study at the university, which offers B.A., M.A., and Ph.D. degrees as well as courses in museum studies. The museum's collections reflect almost a century of work by students and faculty in places as diverse as Africa, Egypt, South Asia, Greece, and the American Southwest. Pre-Columbian and Oceanic works round out the collection.

The museum is wheelchair accessible; there are tours for the visually impaired available without prior notice. Other guided tours can be arranged by calling (314) 882–3591 (at least two weeks in advance for groups).

The **Museum of Anthropology** just re-opened after extensive renovations and now has displays of Native America that are most interesting. Included in the displays are an Arctic fishing village and a pre-pioneer Midwest settlement—a one-room prairie cabin and a fur trader's canoe filled with beaver pelts and ropes of tobacco. Call Molly O'Donnel (314) 882–3764 for more information.

While the museums are easy to find, a well-guarded secret on the university campus is **Bucks Ice Cream,** part of the food and nutrition service. Ice cream and frozen yogurt are made here daily, and it is wonderful stuff. Try their own special Tiger Stripe ice cream. (Just because the nutrition service makes this wonderfully sinful treat doesn't mean it isn't high in butter-fat. It is. But what the heck, it is *sooooo* good.) Richard Linnhardt is the man to talk to about it at (314) 882–1088.

Downtown a new pub and brewery has opened up. The **Flat Branch Pub and Brewery,** needless to say, is very popular with students here. (Students love the homemade root beer and ginger ale.) You can tour the brewing area or have lunch in the pub. Call (314) 499–0400.

Columbia has an active and varied crafts community. **Bluestem Missouri Crafts** (314–442–0211) showcases the work of more than eighty Missouri artists and craftspeople. Whatever your particular weakness, from wrought iron to weaving, from folk-art whirligigs to fine jewelry, you'll find it at Bluestem (named after the native prairie grass, of course); the shop is located at 13 South Ninth Street. Shop 10:00 A.M. till 6:00 P.M. Monday through Saturday, until 8:30 P.M. Thursday night, and noon until 5:00 P.M. on Sunday.

A new gallery, ◆ **Over The Edge,** has recently opened featuring art from the eight contiguous states bordering Missouri. Displayed are clay, pottery, blown glass, and huge wooden bowls. Hours are 10:00 A.M. to 6:00 P.M. Monday through Wednesday, Thursday and Friday nights until 8:30 P.M., and Sunday noon to 5:00 P.M. Around Christmas, the hours are extended.

One more gustatory note—okay, two: truffles and chocolate pizza. You'll find these and too many other rich temptations to mention at **The Candy Factory,** 706 East Broadway. These folks call themselves "your hometown candy makers," but the good news is that even if Columbia isn't your home town, they'll be glad to ship anything you want, nationwide. Use the special order number: (314) 443–8222. You can even buy sugar-free chocolates for those people on restricted diets who still need a treat. Prices seem moderate enough; a holiday gift basket ranges from $12 to $52. Summer hours are 10:00 A.M. to 6:00 P.M. weekdays and from 1:00 to 5:30 P.M. on Saturday; winter hours are 9:00 A.M. to 6:00 P.M. weekdays, 10:00 A.M. to 5:30 P.M. on Saturday, and noon to 5:00 P.M. on Sunday.

Carol Leigh Brack-Kaiser is the talent behind two businesses: ◆ **Carol Leigh's Specialties** and Hillcreek Fiber Studio. Carol Leigh's Specialties was created to market products made by Carol's own hands: handspun yarns and fabrics colored with natural dyes, woven shawls, blankets and wall hangings. Hillcreek Fiber Studio is for teaching. It all began with a spinning class at the nearby university. Spinning led to weaving then to dyeing, which led to advanced studies in fiber arts. Carol began to take her work to living history events and rendezvous where people appreciated the labor and old-world methods of her handmade textiles. Now she sits by her adjustable, triangular-shaped loom which she and her son Carl Spriggs patented and now manufacture at her home at 7001 Hillcreek Road, just outside Columbia. Today she has several classes in spinning special fibers, floor loom, and in the ancient methods of inkle and tablet weaving.

She also conducts classes in Navajo-style weaving and a designer's yarn class. Standing over a simmering vat of wool dye, she produces vibrant colors from indigo; Osage orange (also called hedge apple), which gives vibrant yellows and golds; brazilwood for red, purple, plum, maroon, and burgundy; logwood for lavender and black; cochineal, a bug from Central and South America, for bright reds; madder root for orange-red, and other natural dyes. Carol Leigh asks that you call before you visit, (314-874-2233).

◆ **Trattoria Strata Nova** at 21 North 9th is an elegant spot and a favorite with almost everyone you ask. The food is more northern Italian—not so much pasta, more Continental—almost French. Mike, Cheryl and Rocky are proud of this place and well they should be. But don't bother trying to make reservations. It is strictly first-come, first-served. Lunch is served Tuesday through Friday from 11:30 A.M. until 4:00 P.M. Dinner is from 5:00 until 10:00 P.M. Call (314) 442-8992 for more information.

Formosa Restaurant is upstairs over 913 East Broadway (314-449-3339) and serves seven styles of Chinese cooking. While this little spot is sort of hidden away, plenty of people know about it. Hsiang-Yun Chen is from Taiwan and has been serving food here for about six years. Lunch is served from 11:00 A.M. until 2:00 P.M. Monday though Saturday, dinner is from 4:30 to 9:00 p.m Monday through Thursday, and until 10:00 P.M. on Friday and Saturday nights. There is full bar service.

Missouri's answer to the Hard Rock Cafe—**The 63 Diner**—is just outside of Columbia at 5801 North New Highway 763 (314-443-2331). Bright black, white, and chrome decor, dozens of photos of rock 'n' roll favorites and old movie stars, waitresses in saddle shoes and circle skirts, and the end of that big red '59 Cadillac sticking out of the front wall make the place loaded with atmosphere. The food's every bit as good as you remember, too.

About 11 miles east of Columbia on Highway WW and then some gravel roads, **Patrick Nelson** makes eighteenth- and nineteenth-century reproductions and architectural pieces on his small farm. Using cherry, oak, poplar, walnut, hickory—traditional woods used in American furniture—Nelson can reproduce anything you can show him a picture of, including fireplace mantels and custom molding. He makes doors, bedroom and dining room sets, Windsor chairs, and greenwood country chairs. He can alter pieces to fit modern homes or oversized customers. Call ahead for directions to his shop, which is out back in a shed on the farm. There are usually a few pieces in progress to indicate the caliber of his skill, and you can show him what you have in mind and discuss the price. Call him at (314) 642–7776.

Follow the signs from the Rocheport exit to **Moniteau Creek Pottery** (314–698–4011). Fine handcrafted porcelain and stoneware pottery by John Preus is available in a wide variety of shapes and sizes. Find a deep, generous bowl for popcorn, a teapot for a winter's cup of warmth, jars, and other items.

John—or his representative—is in the shop Wednesdays, Fridays, and Saturdays from 10:00 A.M. until 5:00 P.M., or by appointment anytime.

Rocheport is a good spot to sample the KATY Trail through Missouri's middle; it is among the longest of the nation's growing network of rail-trails and by 1994 will stretch 200 miles from Machens just north of St. Louis to Sedalia 90 miles east of Kansas City. The KATY Trail follows the old Missouri-Kansas-Texas Railroad bed that curves along the north bank of the Missouri River, and one of the most scenic parts of the trail rolls from Rocheport southeast to Jefferson City along a wooded band between the river and the cliffs—sheer limestone walls rising 100 feet above the Muddy Mo. The compacted rock pathway is easy riding even for thin racing tires; the canopy of oak and sycamore trees offers brilliant color in the fall, and the trail is flowered with dogwood and redbud in the spring. Summertime rides lead through kaleidoscopic colors of wildflowers and trumpet vine blossoms fluttering with hummingbirds.

If it's not telling tales out of school, you may want to enroll for a term at the **School House Bed and Breakfast** (314–698–2022) in Rocheport. Innkeepers John and Vicki Ott have restored this big foursquare edifice at Third and Clark streets and made it more inviting than any school we've seen. The three-story school was built in 1914 and served as the area's cultural center for over sixty years.

There are now eight guests rooms, each with its own style; there are even antique bathtubs, sinks, and toilets. The Bridal Suite contains a heart-shaped Jacuzzi. The garden courtyard invites relaxation, and the period reception room is available for meetings, business retreats, and intimate parties. Room rates are from $585 per night and include a hearty country breakfast. Whitehorse Antiques, with ten dealers, is on the lower level of the school.

Craft and antiques shops, the Woodwoman Gallery, the New River City Theater, the Word of Mouth Cafe, and the Rocheport Museum nearby offer the visitor plenty to do "out of school."

The family-owned winery ◆**Les Bourgeois Vineyards** (314–698–3401) welcomes visitors. It is located south of Rocheport on Highway BB, 1 mile north of Interstate 70. Admire a spectacular view of the Missouri River and watch the barges float by as you sample Bordeaux-style wines—plus a generous basket of Missouri sausage, cheese, and fresh fruit. Wine garden hours are noon to sunset, Monday through Saturday; Sunday noon to 6:00 P.M. from March through November, but the winery and sales room are open every day of the year from 11:00 A.M. to 6:00 P.M. Now lunch is served daily except Wednesday and ethnic or regional theme diners are served from 5:30 to 8:30 P.M. on Friday and Saturday.

All this driving makes a body thirsty, but by now you've had enough wine; how about an old-fashioned cherry phosphate? Or maybe a thick, rich malt made with hand-dipped ice cream? Stop by tiny Glasgow, where you'll find ◆**Henderson's,** at 523 First Street, a fifth-generation drugstore on the main drag. They'll fix you the fantasy float of your dreams. Hours are Monday through Friday from 7:00 A.M. until 5:30 P.M., Saturday till 5:00 P.M. and Sunday from 7:00 A.M. until 11:00 A.M. so you have to go right after church or get up very early. (816) 338–2125.

Glasgow's narrow, two-story city hall has a surprised expression; the round-topped windows look like raised eyebrows. But there's nothing too shocking in this historic little town unless you discover that the old bridge on Highway 240 is the world's first all-steel bridge, built in 1878. Eight hundred tons of steel were used in construction at a cost of $500,000; it costs more than that to salt the wintry streets of a small city today.

Near Fayette is the only spot in the entire Western Hemisphere—that's hemisphere, folks—where you'll find inland salt grass. Moniteau Lick, near the more familiar Boone's Lick, is the place. This area was once important for naturally occurring salt; there are more than eighty place-names in Missouri containing the word "salt" or "saline."

GLACIATED PLAINS

Civil War buffs will discover the General Sterling Price Monument by the highway at Keytesville. Farther north you'll pass through a real Mickey Mouse town (Marceline is the birthplace of Walt Disney) on your way to Brookfield. Every Labor Day, hot-air balloon races are held nearby. There's a sustained "swooooosh" as the balloons lift off; it sounds like the sharp intake of the watching crowd's breath, but it's the hot breath of the craft themselves, rising in the morning air. More than fifty balloons join in the fun, filling the sky with crayon-box colors.

From here, a short jaunt westward will take you to Laclede and the ◆ **General John J. Pershing Boyhood Home.** The rural gothic building is a National Historic Landmark and is as ramrod straight as the old man himself, softened with just a bit of gingerbread. The museum highlights Pershing's long career. Only 3 miles away is the Pershing State Park, with the largest remaining wet prairie in Missouri, Late Woodland Indian mounds, and the War Mothers Statue. Also, Locust Creek Covered Bridge State Historic Site is just north of Pershing's home.

Open farmland dominates Highway 5 North; the rolling hills recall the prairie that covered much of presettlement Missouri. Eastward, just outside of Milan discover busy Kirksville and environs. There's a lot happening in Kirksville, as always in a college town. This is the home of Northeast Missouri State University and the Kirksville College of Osteopathic Medicine—lots of lively young things running around here, having fun, eating out, and just generally being college kids.

Is your family doctor an M.D. or a D.O.? If he is a doctor of Osteopathy (D.O.), his profession got its start right here in Kirksville when Andrew Taylor Still established the first school of the osteopathic profession in 1892, in a one-room schoolhouse. The college has grown; today there are fifteen buildings (including two hospitals) on a fifty-acre campus, and the student body numbers more than 500. Former United States Surgeon General C. Everett Koop himself delivered the 1988 commencement address.

Visit the ◆ **Andrew Taylor Still National Osteopathic Museum** at 311 Fourth Street weekdays from 9:00 A.M. till 3:00 P.M. It's a three-building complex that includes the log cabin birthplace of Dr. Still, the tiny, white clapboard cabin that served as the school, and the museum itself, with its impressive collection of osteopathic paraphernalia.

Buildings of many architectural styles, from Romanesque and Renaissance Revival to Italianate and Victorian, from Art Deco and Art Nouveau to Beaux Arts and Prairie, strut their stuff on the walking tour of Old Towne Kirksville. Begin the grand tour at Old Towne Park (Elson and Washington streets) and follow the signs, or pick up a map at any of the businesses marked with a red flag. It's only 1⅛ miles by foot—but well over one hundred years if you're traveling in time.

The Manhattan at 108 South Elson, (816–665–2075) is the longest-established restaurant in northeast Missouri, owned by the same family for three generations. They know what they're doing—nobody stays in business that long without having something on the ball. Try the Athenian salad, gyros, eggplant parmigiana, and best of all, avgolemono soup. (If that's Greek to you, it's an egg-lemon soup that may sound strange but is heaven to the taste buds.) While we're speaking Greek, don't forget a tiny slice of baklava, that phyllo pastry, honey, and nut confection that really is "food for the gods." Hours are 11:00 A.M. to 8:00 P.M. on Sunday and 11:00 A.M. to 9:00 P.M. Tuesday through Saturday. Summer hours are 11:00 A.M. until 2:00 P.M. and 4:30 to 9:00 P.M. Tuesday through Saturday, and on Sunday from 11:00 A.M. until 3:00 P.M.

When the night life gets too much for you in hoppin' Kirksville, head out of town to ❖ **Thousand Hills State Park.** This part of Missouri was sculpted by glaciers; rich, glacial soil is the norm, not the exception, and the streams and rivers that cut through this deep soil formed the "thousand hills."

The park straddles the Grand Divide. Like the Continental Divide, this geologic land form is an area where high ground determines the direction of surface water drainage. It always seems as if you should feel the difference as you cross, but you don't. This mini-mountain ridge runs along Highway 63 from the Iowa-Missouri border to just south of Moberly; western streams and rivers flow into the Missouri River, eastern waters into the Mississippi.

Much of the park is remnant prairie—look for big bluestem, rattlesnake master, blazing star, and Indian grass, which are maintained by periodic burning. Because of the cooler climate here, you'll find plants not found in other parts of the state, such as the lovely interrupted fern in the deep ravines in the park. There is a natural grove of large-toothed aspen, a tree common to northern states but quite rare in Missouri. In Thousand Hills State Park you can find our grand-champion aspen.

If prehistory interests you more than natural history, don't miss the petroglyphs near camping area No. 3. Archaeologists believe these crosses, thunderbirds, sunbursts, and arrows were scratched into the native sandstone by peoples who inhabited the site between A.D. 1000 and 1600. They may have been reminders of the order of the ceremonial rituals passed along by the Middle Mississippi culture, which were in use for a long period of time. Many glyphs appear to have been carved by hunters of the Late Woodland culture between A.D. 400 and 900. The site is listed on the National Register of Historic Places; it's nice to know this list contains more than the usual antebellum mansions and federal-style courthouses we seem to expect.

Take the highway south to Ethel—that is, if you love hand-thrown pottery. This little town is the home of **Clay Images** (816–486–3471). Jim and Melissa Hogenson are well-known artists who work in clay; you may have seen their whimsies—dragons and wizards—at Renaissance festivals around the country. Don't miss this little gold mine (all right, clay mine).

Macon is known all over the state for good antiques shopping. The prices are very reasonable and the shops are full. Start at the largest, **Carrousel Antiques,** at 125 Vine Street (816) 385–4284. Ruth Cordle will show you around the 35 booths in the mall. Hours are 10:00 A.M. until 5:00 P.M. seven days a week.

There are three B&Bs in Macon, too, so if you shop till you drop, you have a choice of places of where to drop.

Just five miles west of Macon in the little coal mining town of Bevier is Al Abadessa's place, ❖**The Pear Tree.** This is a local favorite and people drive from all over the region to eat here. It has a well balanced menu of good old American favorites— steak, lobster, shrimp, chicken and sole—and offers an assortment of wines both by the glass and by the bottle. Do not leave the restaurant without trying the onion rings and save room for an after dinner drink—a Pink Squirrel or a Velvet Hammer—made with their own homemade ice cream. Call (816) 773–6666 for reservations. The Pear Tree is open for dinner Tuesday through

171

Saturday from 5:00 to 10:00 P.M. It is closed during January.

Tiny **Ten Mile** just north of Macon doesn't even show on the map; it's an Amish community near Ethel. Watch for little yard signs; many of these places have tiny shops on the farmstead where baked goods, yard goods, homemade candy, and baskets or quilts are sold.

Take the grand tour through Paris (no, not the long way around; this is Paris, Missouri) to tiny Florida, the closest town to the ◆**Mark Twain Birthplace State Historic Site** (314–565–3449) and Mark Twain State Park, which offers camping, swimming, and river recreation. The two-room cabin where Samuel Clemens came into the world reminds you of something; it could have come straight from one of his books. A bit of Twain was Tom Sawyer and Huck Finn (you remember Huck, that red-haired scamp who lived life to the hilt, devil-take-the-hindmost). If you've read *The Adventures of Huckleberry Finn*, this won't come as a big surprise.

What is a surprise is that the two-room cabin is totally enclosed in an ultramodern museum, which houses first editions of Clemens's works, including the handwritten version of Tom Sawyer done for British publication. Sit in the public reading room to conduct personal research—or just to get in touch with the old wag. For example, Twain once wrote, "Recently someone in Missouri has sent me a picture of the house I was born in. Heretofore I always stated that it was a palace but I shall be more guarded now." There is an admission charge.

Also, the second full weekend of August each year the U. S. Army Corps of Engineers, the Missouri Department of Natural Resources, and the Friends of Florida sponsor the Salt River Folklife Festival in the tiny town of Florida.

◆**Ruffles and Lace,** in Perry at 118 Main, is a neat shop open only on weekends, because owner Sue Dudgeon has just opened a new shop in Hannibal where there is "more traffic." So this off-the-beaten-path shop is uncrowded and a fun spot in which to spend time. Sue has a wonderful selection of decorator items, everything from sophisticate to country at up to 50 percent savings. She carries framed prints, too. This is a very large place. Hours are 10:00 A.M. to 5:00 P.M. on Friday and Saturday, and noon to 8:00 P.M. on Sunday.

Although this is not Madison County, 5 miles west of Paris

and 3 miles south on County Route C, you'll find a different kind of nostalgic symbol, the Union Covered Bridge. You can almost hear the clatter of horses' hooves and the rumble of wagon wheels through the old wooden tunnel. (You'll have to use your imagination; the recently restored bridge is open to foot traffic only; it's blocked to vehicles.) A set of interpretive displays at the unmanned site fills you in on covered bridge history in Missouri. Call the Mark Twain Birthplace at (314) 565–3449 for information and directions to the bridge.

After a picnic at the covered bridge, continue west on Highway 24 to Highway 151. (Pay attention, now.) Go south to Highway M. After a few miles you will come to Highway Y. A drive south on Y will take you through another Amish community. There are no retail shops along the route except maybe Sam's Store, which has no sign out front—you have to ask for directions—but there are signs in the yards offering a variety of handmade goods. The signs advertise homemade candy, quilts and furniture. Fresh garden produce, eggs, and honey are also sold. You can get off the highway and take many small buggy roads to explore the community. Small schools, like the one named Plain View, dot the landscape and buggies leave dust trails on the roads. This is Middle America in its most simple form.

There are some pretty exotic destinations around here, aren't there? Milan, Paris—and now Mexico, south of "gay Paree." Mexico is called "Little Dixie," because of its strong Southern sympathies during the Civil War; now you can visit the Little Dixie Wildlife Area nearby.

Notice all the red brick buildings in the Mexico/Vandalia area? The land is underlaid with a type of refractory clay that makes great bricks; there are still four brick plants in Audrain County.

A 14–mile jog back east from Mexico will take you to Centralia. Don't miss it if you enjoy "kinder, gentler" countryside. ❖ **Chance Gardens** includes a turn-of-the-century mansion, home of the late A. Bishop Chance. Build in 1904, that onion-domed turret, gracious porticoes, and ornate woodwork invite visitors with an eye for elegance. A gift to the public from the A. B. Chance Company (the town's largest industry), it's been Centralia's showplace for years.

The gardens that surround the home say something about the kind of luxury money can't buy. It takes time to plan those masses of color that bloom continuously through the seasons and lead the eye from one brilliant display to another—time to plan and time to maintain. That's a luxury most of us don't have.

Tiny Clark, a hoot and a holler from Centralia, is the birthplace of General Omar Bradley. There's an active Amish community in the Clark area; watch for those horses and buggies. Some sport bumper stickers, much easier to read at this speed than on the interstates. I'M NOT DEAF, I'M IGNORING YOU and I MAY BE SLOW, BUT I'M AHEAD OF YOU seem to be local favorites. You'll want to slow down yourself to admire the clean, white homes and commodious barns of the Amish.

MISSOURI'S MONARCHY

Fulton has played host to Winnie—that's Winston Churchill—who journeyed here to address Westminster College in 1946. Churchill was out of office when he delivered the most famous speech of his life, the "Iron Curtain" speech. "From Stettin in the Baltic to Trieste in the Adriatic, an iron curtain has descended across the Continent. Behind that line lie all the capitals of the ancient states of Central and Eastern Europe...." Those were prophetic words; what would Churchill say now?

The ties between the college, the town, and Great Britain remain unbroken. In the 1960s, Westminster President R.L.D. Davidson wanted to honor those ties. The resulting plan was bold and perfect—if not as well-publicized as the move of the London Bridge to Arizona. The college acquired the Church of St. Mary the Virgin, Aldermanbury, England, and dismantled it stone by stone. The edifice was shipped across the Atlantic and cross-country to Fulton, where it was reconstructed on Westminster campus and rededicated in 1969. It now houses the ❖ **Winston Churchill Memorial and Library** (314–642–3361 or -6648), currently the only center in the United States dedicated to the study of the man and his works. Churchill's original oil paintings (the very public man had a private side, and enjoyed relaxing with his paints), letters, manuscripts, personal family mementoes, and other memorabilia are on display, in addition to the fire-scarred communion plate rescued from the ruins of the church after World War II.

The church itself is deeply historical; built in twelfth-century

London, it was redesigned in 1677 by Sir Christopher Wren, one of the finest architects of the period. Damage caused by German bombs seemed to signal its end until Westminster College stepped in to rescue the building. It is open from 10:00 A.M. to 4:30 P.M. seven days a week. Admission is $2.50; $2.00 for AAA members and senior citizens. Children twelve and under are admitted free.

There is a memorial of a different kind in the same town: the **George Washington Carver Memorial** at 909 Westminster Avenue (314–642–5551) honors the Diamond, Missouri, native and presents information about one of our greatest humanitarians and scientists. The memorial includes a study of black history in Missouri as well. It is open on weekends, and there is a small admission charge.

The Loganberry Inn, a turn-of-the-century Victorian home, offers guests B&B accommodations at 310 West Seventh Street, only a block from Westminster College. Rates are from $50 to $60. Call (314) 642–9229 for more information.

Fulton was also the home of Henry Bellamann, author of *King's Row.* Set in Fulton, the novel was made into a movie in the 1940s starring none other than Missourian Bob Cummings and a pre-presidential Ronald Reagan. The chamber of commerce displays memorabilia from the movie and offers a walking tour of the *King's Row* setting.

Thence, hie thyself back east along Interstate 70 to ◆**Graham Cave State Park** (314–564–3476) near Danville. (Oops, this royalty stuff gets to you!) Graham Cave is a huge, arch of sandstone that dwarfs its human visiors. This rainbow-shaped cave is shallow, so the tour is a self-guided one. Spelunkers, don't let that put you off. Although this is not a deep-earth cave with spectacular formations, artifacts were found here dating from the area's earliest human habitation, some 10,000 years ago. Before the Native Americans formed themselves into tribes, Graham Cave was an important gathering place. Spear-type flints, made before the bow was invented, were found here, along with other signs of human use. The dig itself is fenced to prevent finds from being removed, but you can admire these fine examples of the earliest Show Me State inhabitants in the small museum in the park office. Take the Danville/Montgomery City exit off the interstate and follow Outer Road TT 2 miles west; it dead ends at the park, so you can't go wrong. Check in at the park office to pick up a map to the cave.

Index

Entries for bed and breakfasts, inns, restaurants, and shopping appear in the special indexes beginning on page 181.

177

SPECIAL INDEXES

Shopping

Index